1,001
Ways to Be
CREATIVE

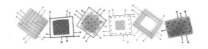

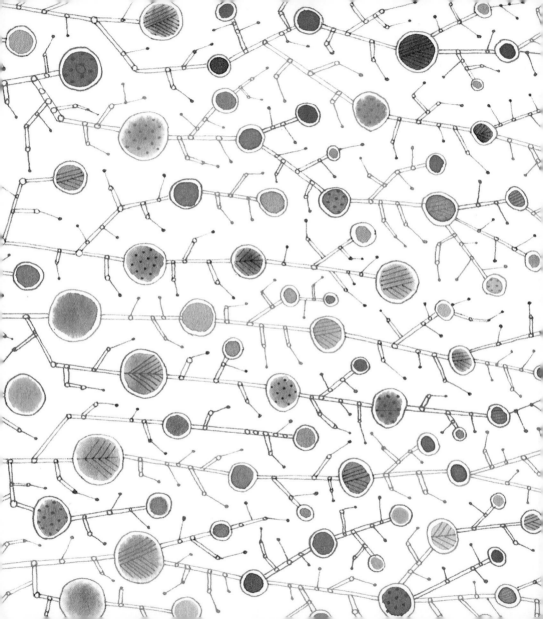

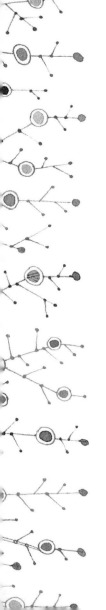

1,001
Ways to Be
CREATIVE

A LITTLE BOOK OF EVERYDAY INSPIRATION

barbara ann kipfer

Illustrations by
Francesca Springolo

NATIONAL
GEOGRAPHIC

Washington, D.C.

Since 1888, the National Geographic Society has funded more than 12,000 research, exploration, and preservation projects around the world. National Geographic Partners distributes a portion of the funds it receives from your purchase to National Geographic Society to support programs including the conservation of animals and their habitats.

National Geographic Partners
1145 17th Street NW
Washington, DC 20036-4688 USA

Get closer to National Geographic explorers and photographers, and connect with our global community. Join us today at nationalgeographic.com/join

For information about special discounts for bulk purchases, please contact National Geographic Books Special Sales: specialsales@natgeo.com

For rights or permissions inquiries, please contact National Geographic Books Subsidiary Rights: bookrights@natgeo.com

Library of Congress Cataloging-in-Publication Data

Names: Kipfer, Barbara Ann, author.
Title: 1,001 ways to be creative : a little book of everyday inspiration / Barbara Ann Kipfer ; illustrations by Francesca Springolo.
Other titles: One thousand and one ways to be creative
Description: Washington, D.C. : National Geographic, [2017]
Identifiers: LCCN 2017040298 | ISBN 9781426219078
Subjects: LCSH: Creative ability. | Creative thinking.
Classification: LCC BF408 .K545 2017 | DDC 153.3/5--dc23
LC record available at https:// lccn.loc.gov_2017040298

Printed in China

17/RRDS/1

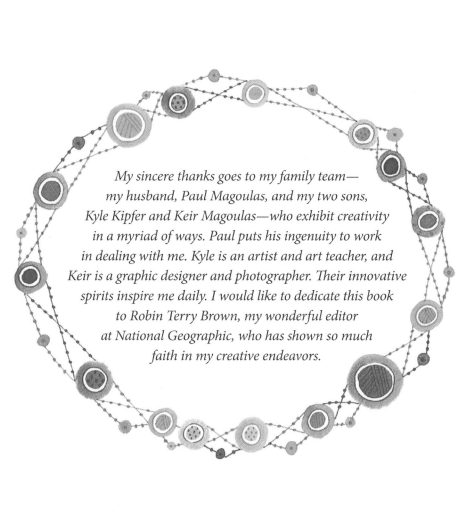

*My sincere thanks goes to my family team—
my husband, Paul Magoulas, and my two sons,
Kyle Kipfer and Keir Magoulas—who exhibit creativity
in a myriad of ways. Paul puts his ingenuity to work
in dealing with me. Kyle is an artist and art teacher, and
Keir is a graphic designer and photographer. Their innovative
spirits inspire me daily. I would like to dedicate this book
to Robin Terry Brown, my wonderful editor
at National Geographic, who has shown so much
faith in my creative endeavors.*

Introduction

The creative instinct is an enormous superenergy. It is that inexplicable burst of inspiration that suddenly allows you to see from a new angle or bring something new into existence. The power of novelty interrupts the "usual" and induces you to action.

Most people crave the joy of letting their brains roam free, unencumbered by deadlines and schedules. We delight in working with our hands, get a thrill out of creating something beautiful, and yearn to indulge our interests and passions.

But that creative spark can be elusive as our day-to-day responsibilities and routines overtake novelty.

The first step to becoming more creative is to give yourself permission to spend time on these "frivolous" pursuits. You will be amazed at how this indulgence will improve the quality of your life and relationships.

In *1,001 Ways to Be Creative*, the third book in my 1,001 Ways series, you will find energizing ideas and tips for bringing more creativity into your life. Whether your passion is music, art, dance, writing, or theater—or if you are still seeking the creative outlet that is right for you—this book speaks to all who seek greater creativity in their lives. I also share thought-provoking quotes and lists that will help lead you to inspiration. Dip in anywhere and see where each page takes you.

Creativity isn't only about artistic skills; it is a way of seeing the world. It gives you the power to shape your life, unify and balance your interests, and emphasize your uniqueness. What is your recipe for creativity? It's all about what makes you YOU.

1
Play.

2
Make a miniature version of anything.

3
Design a family crest. You can even
include your pet.

4
Find an intriguing item in an antique store
and seek out its history.

5

Do not look for an audience, admiration,
or validation right away. Create for yourself first.

6

For one day, bestow a unique and truthful
compliment on each person you see.

7

Reflect on the people who have stirred
your creativity. Is it possible to re-create
that inspiration by yourself?

8

Teach your unique knowledge of something.

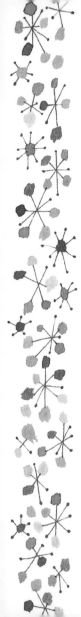

9

Sketch interesting architecture.
Note the features that reflect the whim
of the architect.

10

Get over trying to be completely unique. You are
a mash-up of all your experiences and ideas.

11

Don't quit too soon.

12

True art is inspired by the heart.
Pay attention to how you feel.

13

Intimidated by a blank page? Write down
a line from a favorite song and then write
an entirely new song to follow it.

14

Design a magazine cover.

15

Get out of your comfort zone.
New experiences spark creative ideas.

16

Write about the most meaningful thing
you did as a child.

17

Be persistent. It takes time to develop new skills.

18

The greatest pleasure is usually in the making,
not the end product.

19

Think outside the box every day. Drive a new
route home from work or have a barbecue
for Christmas dinner.

20

Make a rock garden.

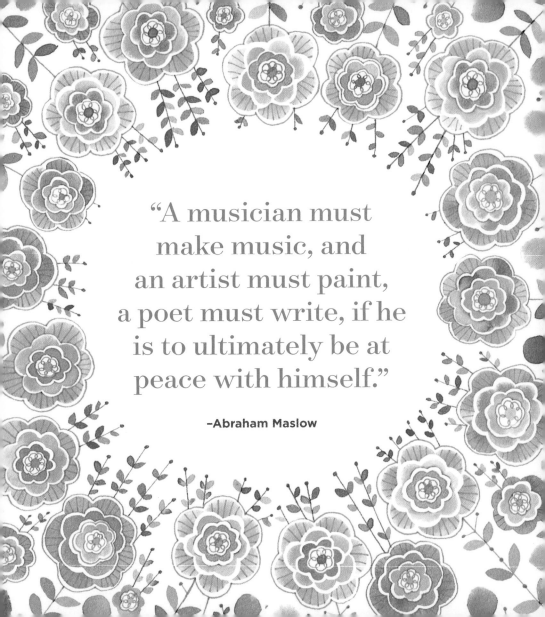

"A musician must make music, and an artist must paint, a poet must write, if he is to ultimately be at peace with himself."

–Abraham Maslow

21

Sketch a self-portrait using a photo
as a guide.

22

Keep up your momentum.

23

Eat ice cream for breakfast. Small pleasures
spark joy and creativity.

24

Make today the first day of your
new hobby.

25

Color in the empty spaces of a crossword.

26

Ask yourself if you would like to learn
a new skill.

27

Use creative visualization at night
as you fade off to sleep.

28

Carve a watermelon into an edible sculpture.

29
Make a Wikipedia page about a topic
that no one has entered.

30
Plate your dinner with flair using colorful foods
and a whimsical swizzle of sauce.

31
Acknowledge the times when you have
stood up for an idea you believed in.

32
Tap into your inner strength.

33

Think about what you could be doing instead of watching television or posting on Facebook.

34

Paint the concept of empathy.

35

Creativity is the ability to bring something new into existence.

36

Work on an idea constantly until it is resolved.

Inspirations

Stretch Outside Your Comfort Zone

Go to a poetry slam.

Get lost on purpose and don't use GPS to get back.

Expand your group of acquaintances.

See an avant-garde theater production.

Take an improv class.

Hop on a scary theme park ride.

Watch different TV shows.

Live in the real world instead of binge-watching "reality" shows.

Learn a computer program you previously found daunting.

Phone someone who you only communicate
with electronically.

Join a new community group.

Try a different ethnic food.

Find a physical hobby, such as dance, tai chi, or biking.

Volunteer to help people less fortunate than yourself.

Check out different news sources than your usual fare.

Read a book about a topic you know nothing about.

Acquire a taste for a food you've hated since you were a kid.

When you encounter a word you do not know, look it up.

Create a concrete goal, like running a marathon or writing
a novel, that requires many smaller, incremental goals.

Do balancing exercises throughout the day, like brushing
your teeth while standing on one foot.

37
Channel negative feelings into
a positive creative outlet.

38
Practice stream-of-consciousness writing.
Don't judge, just write nonstop for 15 minutes.

39
Rearrange the art in your house.

40
If you want to do something, find a way to do it.

41

Take a meditative walk. Instead of thinking,
concentrate on the motions of your feet.
Physically slowing down helps promote
divergent thinking, improves your mood,
and can get the creative juices flowing.

42

Pay close attention to your experiences.
You may be able to use what you learn
in creative ways.

43

Sketch for 10 minutes every day.

44

If you get stuck on a project, write a review
of your work. Examine the steps taken so far,
the steps still needed for completion,
and the changes you'd like to make.
Then get back to work.

45

Think about how a more creative approach
at work can benefit you and your employer.

46

Toy with a new idea. Examine it from all angles
and see how its definition changes.

47

Make a list of the creative skills you want
to learn and a list of those you already have
that could use fine-tuning.

48

Don't beat yourself up if you don't have
enough time to spend on your creative pursuits.
Keep showing up and take satisfaction
in your perseverance.

49

Self-development is key to satisfaction
in creative pursuits.

"The unlike is joined together, and from differences results the most beautiful harmony."

–Heraclitus

50

Look at a situation in your life that you know should change. Try looking at it from completely different angles than you have previously. A creative approach may be the jolt you need.

51

Invent a bedtime story.

52

Seek out knowledge from schools, mentors, experts, media, nature, arts, sciences, and philosophy. You will discover everything is connected and interdisciplinary.

53

The challenge each day is to be creative
regardless of the conditions.

54

Dare to apply creative thinking in
an "uncreative" field of endeavor.

55

Paint something in your house
that could use a face-lift.

56

Approach every project with a "let's see
what happens" attitude.

57
Learn to laugh at yourself.

58
Pretend you are the ruler of the world.

59
Keep a notebook of creative epiphanies.

60
Make notes about what would be fun
to draw or write about.

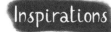

Inspirations

Make a Wish List for the Future

I have always dreamed of living in _____.

I am dying to write a book about _____.

If I were to give a commencement speech, it would begin with _____.

I would like to make enough money to _____.

I have always wanted to learn to _____.

In my lifetime, I want to experience _____.

I wish I could make a difference in _____.

I would like to be doing more of _____.

I could see myself being friends with_____.

I look forward to discovering _____.

If I could travel to only one place, it would be _____.

61

Find an object from your childhood
and turn it into a piece of artwork.

62

Churn your own butter.

63

Ride the waves, ebbs and flows, questions
and answers, or flashes of insight and see
where they take you.

64

Enter an unusual competition to test
your limits.

65
Write about the most expensive thing you
ever bought, other than a house or car.

66
Set up an easel on the veranda
of a grand hotel and paint.

67
Write a sonnet.

68
Often the best way to learn is to go to a person
who does something well and study their work.

69
Build a wigwam.

70
Plant a garden to experience the joy of creating life with your own two hands.

71
Alter your perceptions: turn an object upside down and stare at it, wear earplugs, or walk mindfully instead of at your normal pace.

72
What do you create when there is quiet and solitude?

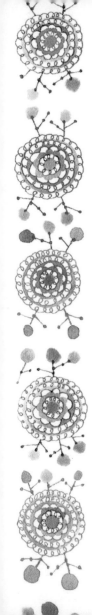

73
Don't just look, see. Practice looking with penetration at least once per hour.

74
Learn by copying.

75
Take something apart and put it back together. You will learn that the object is actually more than the sum of its parts.

76
Aim for discovery—look at the same thing as everyone else and think something different.

"A routine creates
a landing place
for the muse."

–Alex Soojung-Kim Pang

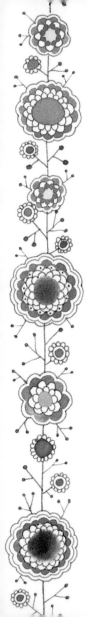

77

When was the last time you did something
for the first time?

78

Sing every word of a grand opera.

79

How can you be more spontaneous?

80

Help build a children's playground.

81

Watch the movie *Field of Dreams,*
then figure out what you want to build.

82

Create a Mr. Potato Head out of real vegetables.

83

Paint a picket fence.

84

Have a backward spelling bee.

85

Forget what other people think of your efforts, how you compare with others, and whether what you achieve will be "good enough."

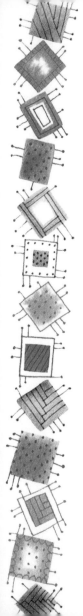

86

Design your own tattoo.

87

Make a family activity calendar.

88

Play alphabet charades (spell with your body).

89

Identify a big dream that is doable but will
require your particular talents.

90

Draw a political cartoon.

91

Use the panorama setting on your phone
to take an epic photo.

92

Your creativity will flourish as you practice
risktaking, perseverance, and openness
to experience.

93

Dig deep into your basic assumptions.
Which of them should be dropped?

94

Create delightful children's rooms.

95
Design a skateboard.

96
Expand beyond the solutions you
have used in the past.

97
Make a file of all your favorite quotes, passages
from books, and movie lines. They may provide
inspiration for a creative project.

98
Give yourself the free time you need
to explore.

Reflect on Your Creative History

Write a history or time line of your creative accomplishments.

Note the five projects that stand out.

What are the shared features of the five projects you chose?

What was the preparation stage?

How did you solve any problems or jump any hurdles?

Did you have a creative "aha" moment?

In the end, how did you feel about what you created?

Could you tweak your idea to make it better?

For the projects that you considered a success,
what did you do with the finished work?

For the projects that you considered a failure,
what did you do with them?

What would you like to do now?

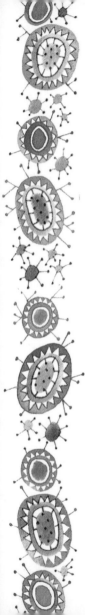

99

Take a picture out of the same window every day for a month. Notice how the scene varies as the sunlight shifts, nature changes, and your neighbors' lives move along.

100

Draw an aerial view of your home.

101

Fill an entire coloring book.

102

Wear silly socks.

103

Enjoy your creative work and let success come naturally.

104

Draw sadness.

105

Start an innovative collection.

106

Make lists of what you like—and why.

107

Create an inspiration corner in your home.

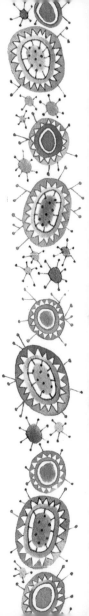

108

Changing your patterns of behavior
can spur creativity.

109

Contribute something to the world
that only you can offer.

110

Record your ideas—then realize how many
good ones you have.

111

List 10 words describing your current project.
Look them up in a thesaurus, then gain inspiration
by adding a synonym for each to the list.

112

Design a quilt pattern.

113

Make a sundial.

114

Take up wood carving.

115

Create your own trail mix.

116

Turn a children's song into
a picture book.

"As irrigators lead water where they want, as archers make their arrows straight, as carpenters carve wood, the wise shape their minds."

–The Buddha

117
Write a letter to the editor of your local paper.

118
Write an animal fable.

119
Watch a bud open.

120
Paint faces at a child's birthday party.

121
Create an atmosphere that welcomes your creativity and kindles your joy.

122
Read op-ed pages for ideas.

123
Nurture others' creativity by being more
supportive than critical. Praise the strengths
of a work in progress.

124
Come up with a vanity license plate
that describes you.

125
Dream about building a colony on Mars.

126

Images and visualization are the language of your unconscious, where creative ideas form.

127

Grow corn in the backyard.

128

Capture a moving moment on camera.

129

Write a great love story.

130

Make a stencil pattern.

Discover Your Authentic Self

What are five things you can do?

What are five things you cannot do?

As a child, what did you want to be when you grew up?
Is that interest still relevant to you?

What was the most creative or exciting place
you ever worked?

What makes you laugh?

What do you like that your mother liked?

What do you like that your father liked?

What do you dislike that your mother disliked?

What do you dislike that your father disliked?

Who truly accepts you as you are?

Are you more creative when alone
or with others?

How does your mood affect your
creative output?

What is your greatest creative ability or gift?
Do others recognize it?

Who is your muse?

Whose muse are you?

In what part of your life are you
most creative now?

In what part of your life would you like
to be more creative?

131

Invent something with as many uses as Velcro.

132

Learn to sew.

133

Create a happy family life.

134

Make a big batch of Rice Krispies treats
with creative fillings.

135

Create a secret handshake.

136

Exploring can bring serendipitous ideas.
Stay awake and aware.

137

Write the book you want to read.

138

Draw what you want to see.

139

Write the music you want to hear.

140

Build a gingerbread house.

141

Study the life and works of a favorite artist.

142

Clear up the small tasks that are distracting you from your project.

143

Come up with 10 alternate uses for any object.

144

Choreograph a performance piece.

145
Solve a Rubik's Cube.

146
Experiment (safely) with a chemistry set.

147
Draw happiness.

148
Treat yourself to a romantic dinner for one
and bring along a sketchbook.

"Creativity is allowing yourself to make mistakes. Art is knowing which ones to keep."

–Scott Adams

149

Write about yourself at 80.

150

Make a list of all the memorable artworks
you have seen in your life.

151

Carve out a space to do your art and impose
some temporary solitude there.

152

Illustrate every item on a list with
a line drawing.

153

Write in detail about something unusual
that happened to you. This might allow you
to see the event in a more imaginative way.

154

Can you write a better ending to a bad movie?

155

Make paper airplanes.

156

Create family rituals that become traditions.

Inspirations

Start a Journal of Ideas

Write down all ideas for new projects. Do not edit yourself. You can refine the list later.

Save meaningful quotes.

Note the interesting and strange things that happen every day.

Sketch out your ideas.

List the books you would like to read.

Create menus for your week or a fabulous dinner party—real or imagined.

Make up a new recipe.

Save facts and trivia that wow you.

Capture your philosophies about life.

Write down topics you want to know more about.

List the things you are grateful for. Reread this list daily.

157
Design colorful geometric shapes and
patterns like the artist Piet Mondrian.

158
Dress up as a storybook character
for Halloween.

159
Prepare a treasure hunt for a birthday party.

160
Construct a waterslide.

161
Design a chandelier.

162
Write a comedy.

163
Draw things that frighten you.

164
Start an inventor's notebook. Let necessity drive your ideas.

165

There is no creativity without some
downtime. Let incubation work.

166

If you are a night owl, experiment with
writing, drawing, painting, or composing
after everyone else has gone to bed.

167

Reread favorite passages and chapters
when seeking inspiration.

168

It's a rainy Sunday afternoon. What do you do?

169
Join a drum circle.

170
Create an imaginary place by piecing together digital snapshots in Photoshop.

171
Failing is a part of any creative pursuit.

172
People with high creative output know what time their minds start firing up and structure their days accordingly.

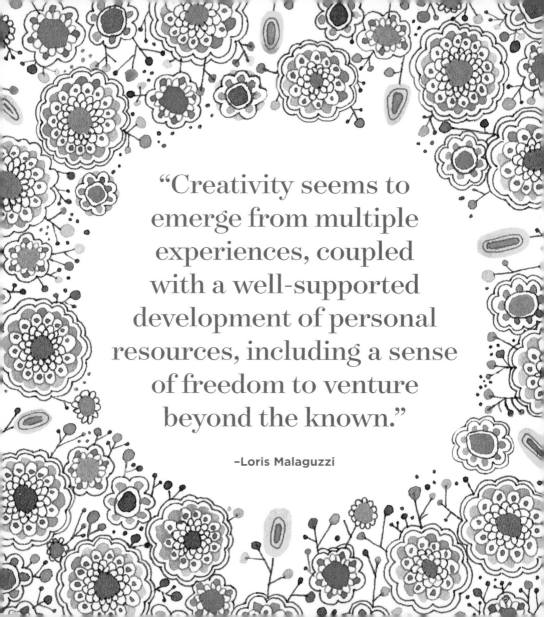

"Creativity seems to emerge from multiple experiences, coupled with a well-supported development of personal resources, including a sense of freedom to venture beyond the known."

–Loris Malaguzzi

173

Invent stories about the people around you during your commute.

174

Focus your commitment and energy on the project you are doing now. Write down all the "someday" ideas for later.

175

Pretend you are Andy Warhol and turn everyday objects into pop art.

176

Come up with new words to a tune.

177
Build a driftwood beach shack.

178
Design your kitchen so that everything
you really need is within reach.

179
Paint a sidewalk mosaic.

180
Pretend you are a scribe and take notes
on the world around you.

181

Create the karma (causes) of happiness (effects).

182

Adopt a shelf at the library and
read everything on it.

183

Think of yourself as a superhero for a day.
How does your behavior change?

184

Creativity is like a tree, extending roots to
draw in nourishment from experience,
which helps to sprout ideas.

185

Turn off the telephone and other devices
during your sacred creative time.

186

Try writing with your nondominant hand.

187

Observing details is worth the effort.
You never know when a particular detail
will be just the inspiration you need.

188

The world is a creative person's oyster—
we see possibilities everywhere.

189

Go to a museum and spend an hour with a painting you have never seen before.

190

Paint your old dinnerware.

191

Make a rain barrel.

192

Draw a Greek temple.

193

Paint pictures of wildflowers.

Make Time for Play

Emulate children's behaviors that cultivate creativity,
such as exploration and playing make-believe.

Spark your imagination by getting ideas
from other places.

Follow your passions.

Take note of what makes an impact on you.

Be willing to experiment.

Follow any curiosity you have and be creative
in pursuing that curiosity.

Add humor and whimsy at times when they
are really needed.

Pursue activities that spark your imagination.

Follow your curiosity.

Seek out situations where you will make discoveries,
such as traveling to a foreign country or hiking
an unfamiliar trail.

Find new uses for ordinary things.

Make a game out of being someplace you do not
want to be. When you are on a crowded airplane,
put on your headphones, crank up your favorite music,
and pretend you are at a concert.

Search online for new bucket list ideas.
Look for things you may not have thought
of on your own.

To make sure you have time to achieve your goal,
schedule time just for play.

194

Develop your own recipe for barbecue sauce.

195

If you are feeling anxious, do a breathing exercise or meditation in a comfortable spot. Then revisit what you are creating.

196

Can you think of 10 or more things that kids do better than adults? Why is that?

197

Make food art. See broccoli as trees, olives as eyes, sugar as snow. You'll never look at your food the same way again.

198

Jot down ideas and insights when they pop up. Notetaking gives the creative process time to breathe.

199

Give yourself permission to be imperfect.

200

Ask yourself, How can I make this moment fun?

201

Play Name That Tune.

202

Amass a body of work one day at a time.

203
Develop your own eccentricity.

204
Who are your influences?

205
A free-range brain meanders, roams,
and wanders. It creates new ideas
and new worlds.

206
Make a conscious effort to introduce
positive change into your life.

207

Good artists figure out their strengths and learn how to circumvent their weaknesses.

208

Create posters to hold up in a cheering section.

209

Make up the rules as you go.

210

Being creative starts from within. It has little to do with outer circumstances or people.

211

Get an ugly Christmas tree instead of a perfect one.
Show it love with fat colored lights, homemade
ornaments, and popcorn strings.

212

Leave a funny note on someone's car windshield.

213

Be open to whatever comes, just as it is.
Do not try to change it or grasp it.

214

Do you have a sanctuary where most
of your "magic" happens?

215
Say "yes, and" rather than "yes, but."

216
Dry summer flowers for winter bouquets.

217
Look, and keep looking until the details
of the world slowly reveal themselves.

218
Make a video about whatever strikes your fancy.

219
Take time for yourself.

220
Volunteer for archaeology digs in your area.
Learning about past cultures may spur
new ways of looking at the world.

221
Design a monument to your hero or heroine.

222
Practice experiencing without thinking.
Can you observe without commentary?

"It took me
a whole lifetime
to paint
like a child."

–Pablo Picasso

223

Spend a day documenting all the patterns you see.

224

Find 10 things that form a circle and
take a photo of each. Perhaps you can
frame each circular object.

225

If you don't have patience with your current
creative project, try a different one.

226

Creative work comes from passion not practicality.

227
What photograph most inspires you?

228
Do the activities that energize you.

229
Try going to bed and waking up an hour earlier. What effect does this have on your projects?

230
Draw your favorite outfit.

231

Find a comfortable seat outside and draw
what is right in front you. Sit in the same place
and draw the same scene in each season.

232

Sketch your future.

233

Build a wishing well in the backyard.

234

Design your dream master bedroom:
size, shape, furniture and its placement,
decorations, windows, everything.

Practice Seeing Like an Artist

Describe how your favorite painting creates a feeling.

Imagine how changes to the colors, composition, and size would affect how you feel about the painting.

Squint your eyes to see the basic shapes—circles, rectangles, squares, and triangles—that make up the work.

Practice looking for these basic shapes in your environment.

Notice the textures around you.

Visit a window in your home at different times of day. Observe how the lighting changes at sunrise, noon, and dusk.

Turn an object upside down and draw it. This will help you see the lines and shapes that make up the whole.

Look for beauty in a piece of art that you think of as ugly.

235
Invent your own hieroglyphics.

236
Create art with the one you love.

237
Dress up and make a fancy dinner at home.

238
Start a patchwork quilt during the year
of your child's birth. Give the finished product
as a high school graduation gift.

239

Rely on intuition rather than intellect.

240

Respect the irrational.

241

If going to a museum inspires you to paint,
act on the feeling before it subsides.

242

When you cannot sleep, create unique
characters in your mind.

243

Look back on your life's passions and see
connections. Maybe everything you have
been passionate about will start
to make sense to you.

244

Take a class in life drawing.

245

When you get immersed in a project and are
suddenly able to put your entire self into it—
sometimes called "flow"—you have found
your true voice.

246
Do self-ethnography, documenting
your own life and culture.

247
Meditation can help turn off the noise
and empty your mind.

248
Make clever anniversary gifts based on
traditional materials for each year,
such as wood, paper, cotton, or flowers.

249
Make a chef's hat.

"First say to yourself
who you wish to be;
and then do accordingly
what you are doing."

–Epictetus

250

Decorate with wine corks.

251

The creative mind explores whatever
it is fascinated by.

252

Awareness becomes vision and expression.

253

Creativity is more about being brave
than having "talent."

254

Limit your options. Sometimes having
too many choices gets in the way.

255

Be an explorer of the world. Wherever you go,
ideas are waiting to be discovered.

256

Create your wedding album.

257

Begin where you are, starting over every morning.

258
Hunt for fossils.

259
Write a movie review.

260
Create a personal gift for someone you love.

261
Using materials you already have forces you to figure out how to put them to good use.

262
Envision an art deco painting.
Then put a brush to canvas.

263
Build your perfect library of books.

264
Ponder why there is so much blue in the world
but almost no blue food.

265
Try to go through an entire day without
spending any money.

266
Be creative with your time.

267
Sometimes the greatest big idea is found
in the marriage of two small ideas.

268
Play a word game like Scrabble to keep
your brain nimble.

269
Do something risky when
the opportunity arises.

270

How could you alter an old item of clothing
to make it new and wearable?

271

Decorate a birthday cake with
an explosion of color.

272

Plot your mood every day. After a month or so,
look for a pattern. Think about ways
to swing negatives into positives.

273

Take a picture of yourself in the same spot each year.

274

Create things for others to make
them feel special.

275

Change the order of your meals for one day.

276

Think of an "accident" as an answer
in search of a different question.

277

Pretend that you lost your voice and
enjoy saying nothing all day.

Inspirations

Allow Yourself to Ask "What If?"

What if people did not need sleep?

What if reincarnation could be confirmed?

What if you could remember everything you read,
heard, or saw?

What if every person was kind all the time?

What if another advanced species existed?

What if you only ate one type of food?

What if there were no seasons?

What if the universe were a giant simulation or dream?

What if we have to move to the oceans or another
planet someday?

What if you did a creative project every day?

278

Give yourself a mini-vacation from
your creative project but keep
a notebook handy.

279

Try to identify the ingredients of
a complex exotic dish.

280

Take a mutual 24-hour break from
your significant other to allow both hearts
to grow fonder. Pledge to invent a new activity
to do together when you reconnect.

281

What forms of creativity come to you easily?
Which ones are a struggle?

282

Indulge daydreams as a way to explore
other modes of thinking.

283

Make a list of three or four fun things you and your
partner have "been meaning to do." Devise a scheme
for doing at least one in the next six months.

284

Take pride in your progress.

285
You learn more while looking for an answer
than in the moment of finding it.

286
The best way to have a good idea is
to have a lot of ideas.

287
A distinctive style comes from experimentation,
play, and practice.

288
Whip together powerful words and dramatic type
to create an impactful work of art.

289
Cut up a piece of art that isn't working.
Sometimes it is best to start from scratch.

290
Recognize novelty and freshness in the familiar.

291
Instead of seeing everyday objects and events
as small, ordinary, and insignificant, see them
as precious, unique, and beautiful.

292
Sit on the floor and play with a toy.

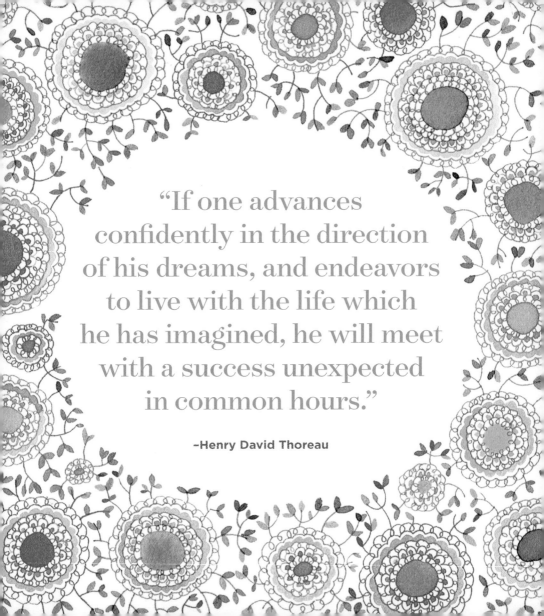

"If one advances
confidently in the direction
of his dreams, and endeavors
to live with the life which
he has imagined, he will meet
with a success unexpected
in common hours."

–Henry David Thoreau

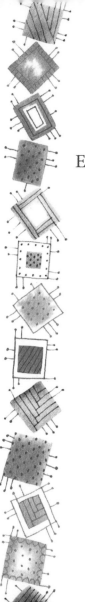

293
Eliminate internal conflict by figuring out your goals, time commitments, and strategies for creating.

294
Blend a unique milkshake flavor.

295
You will be amazed at what you can teach yourself. Be a lifelong learner.

296
Keep your day job. Being able to pay the bills keeps away the top stress producer.

297

If you have a routine, you can figure out
how to slot in creative time.

298

Go to your local bookstore and read one chapter
of several books. Buy the one you like best.

299

Try to work the hours that work for you.

300

Always question why things are the way they are.

301

Think of ways to make current projects
more playful.

302

Appreciate failures as much as successes.

303

Recruit a mentor.

304

If you are having trouble creating,
try *un*creating. Break down the project
into its smallest parts.

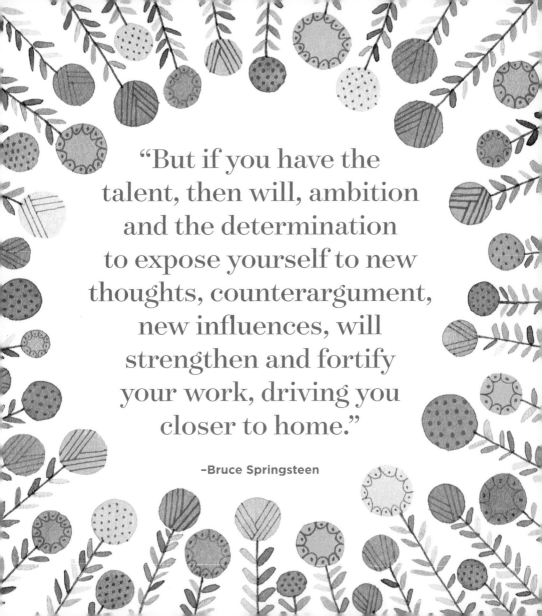

"But if you have the talent, then will, ambition and the determination to expose yourself to new thoughts, counterargument, new influences, will strengthen and fortify your work, driving you closer to home."

–Bruce Springsteen

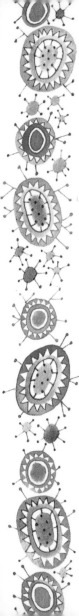

305
Take two very different things and conjure
a connection between them.

306
Enter the whimsical land of reverie.

307
Paint a beautiful landscape.

308
Remember that there is no "right" way.

309
When you are seeking new ideas, go for a walk.

310
Create a bed for your pet.

311
Write up a problem or project like a recipe.
The recipe should contain essential
ingredients and also "spices."

312
Read collections of "best stories."
They may jog your imagination.

313
Design sets for your community theater.

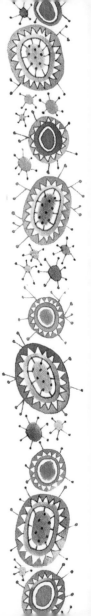

314

Draw a piece of furniture as you are
looking down on it. Then draw it while you're
underneath looking up, and from the side.

315

While gazing upon a beautiful landscape,
compose a perfect photograph in your mind
before trying to shoot it.

316

Sing your favorite hymn loudly in a church full
of people, sing karaoke, sing the blues in the shower,
sing along with the radio when you drive.
Sing anywhere that makes you happy.

317

Get obsessed with your art.

318

Keep several irons in the fire. Do not invest
your whole self in one project.

319

Close your eyes and for 20 seconds connect
to a place inside that is undisturbed
by anyone or anything.

320

Learn to trust the beauty that you sense
in a good idea.

Build What's in Your Imagination

An archaeological model

A bead loom

A beautiful dollhouse
with real electric lights

A bed frame

A birdhouse
(see if a bird comes)

A bookcase

A brick barbecue

A cabin in the woods

A catapult

A collage

A dream house with
Lincoln Logs

A dry stone wall

An elaborate construction
of Popsicle sticks

A fallout shelter

A fire pit or fireplace

A fort with blankets

A grape arbor

A haunted dollhouse

A home weather station

A leaf house

A miniature golf course
with soup cans

A model

An obstacle course

A puppet stage

A robot

A sandcastle with
a moat and canal

A scarecrow

A secret compartment
inside your desk

A secret hideaway

A shrine

A snow fort

A spaceship

A tabletop terrarium

A tarp shelter

A tiny house

A totem pole

A town of Lego blocks

A window garden

A wooden table

A Zen rock garden

321

Everyone is creative. We all generate ideas,
but only a few act on those ideas. Fear is
often what holds us back.

322

Stroll along a street that you have
never seen before.

323

Find someone to be your sounding board.

324

Paint the walls of your mind with
many beautiful pictures.

325

Experiment with a kitchen herb garden.
Build meals around the plants that
are growing the fastest.

326

Write a poem and post it in a public place
for others to enjoy.

327

Collect only what you love.

328

Study the artist, musician, or writer you
most admire. Learn everything about the
person and what he or she has created.

329

Make an inspiration board of favorite magazine
clippings, photos, fabric swatches, works of art,
or anything that brings you joy.

330

Creative learners reflect on their own
learning process.

331

Brainstorm a problem, writing three new solutions
each day for a week. At the end of the week,
choose the most promising plan of action.

332

Press flowers.

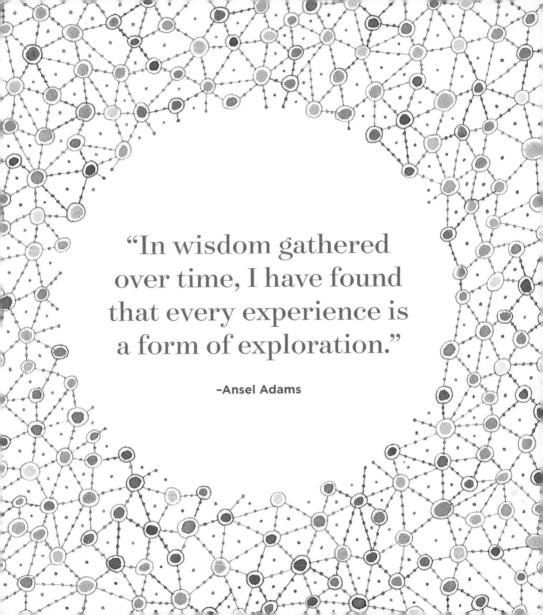

"In wisdom gathered over time, I have found that every experience is a form of exploration."

–Ansel Adams

333
Draw your ideal living room.

334
Sign up for a course in something
completely impractical.

335
Remember that nothing is original.

336
Record sounds, textures, tastes, and smells.

337
Write about a meal that you have
never forgotten.

338

Ask questions, make mistakes, and acknowledge your doubts. These are ways to learn and create something new.

339

Notice what light does to objects at different times of day.

340

Paint a giant mural with a group of friends.

341

Let ideas incubate. Time can help separate workable ideas from ones that should be set aside.

342
Watch a quiz show and try to answer
every question. Dig deep in your memory.

343
Learn something new every day.

344
What would you like to leave as your creative legacy?

345
Delve into the study of design in nature,
called teleology.

346
Imagine ordinary everyday scenes as photographs.

347
Train yourself to notice details as soon
as you enter a new space.

348
Draw the space surrounding an object,
not the object itself. What do you see?

349
Paint joy.

350
Write from the heart.

351
Doubt the things that others take for granted.

352
Creativity is a cycle of preparation, incubation,
insight, evaluation, and elaboration.
Try documenting these stages.

353
Dress out of character for a day.
Then write about the experience.

354
Throw a themed birthday party for your partner.

355
Take note of at least five things you see right now
that you have never noticed before.

356
Ask a stupid question.

357
Spend some time every weekend creating,
constructing, or renovating something.

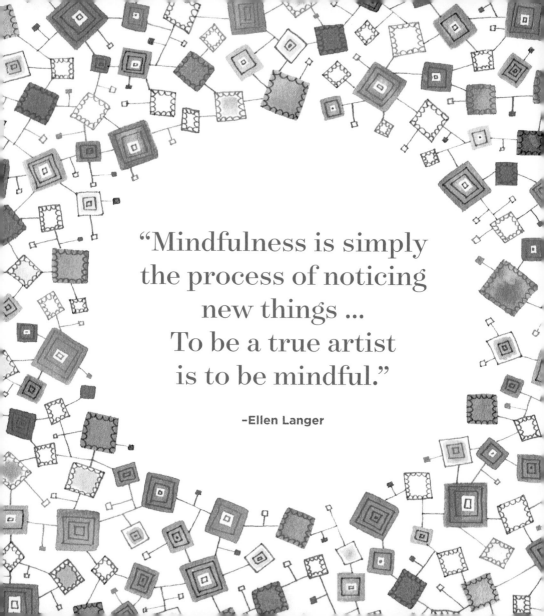

"Mindfulness is simply
the process of noticing
new things ...
To be a true artist
is to be mindful."

–Ellen Langer

358

Play music that matches your mood.

359

Designate a drawing or painting wall
where you create whatever you want;
you can always paint over it later.

360

It takes time to develop a unique
creative voice or style.

361

Practice deep looking and deep listening.

362

Limited funds can encourage creative solutions.

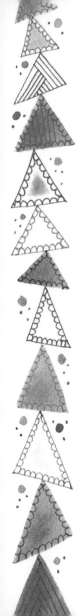

363

Expand your awareness to the edges
of your visual field.

364

Form a family band using homemade instruments.

365

Wear a blindfold and describe something
using only your sense of touch.

366

Scribble ideas on napkins or scraps of paper when
they come to you. Don't let them escape!

367
Solitude can be the key to producing
your best work.

368
Make a fabulous soup from ingredients
you have in the kitchen right now.

369
Start your own pillow book, a traditional
Japanese journal in which you write
unrelated notes about dreams, experiences,
observations, and ideas.

370

Create a vision statement for your creative life, wherever it stands right now. What would you like to acquire, grow, develop, and nurture?

371

You can learn something from every experience.

372

Lose your fear of being wrong.

373

Never become an expert. Look at everything as if you have never seen it before. Approach each task as if you are doing it for the first time.

374

Get your rough draft and raw ideas
out of your head as soon as possible.
Then build on the parts you like.

375

Draw things that make you happy.

376

Believe in yourself and your work. If you don't,
how can you expect anyone else to?

377

Make a sand painting, your own mandala.

378

Be proud to be different.

Take Yourself on a Creativity Field Trip

Go to a museum or gallery. Choose a room and study each painting in it.

Read the descriptions for each piece.

Listen to the audio tour if one is available.

Think about which painting you would like to own.

Describe that painting in words.

Why does this painting appeal to you?

What questions about the painting and the artist does this work bring to mind?

Notice how colors, lines, shapes, and textures contribute to the overall effect of the work.

Seek out a docent who can discuss the painting with you.

379

What doodads and treasures have you collected that inspire you?

380

Produce an amateur documentary.

381

Think about the compliments you have received that made you feel good about your talents.

382

Which musicians do you love? What does their music inspire in you?

383

Start a "million-dollar idea" list of new
and improved products.

384

Experiment with different signatures
for signing your work.

385

Take a series of photographs of one scene
over the course of a year.

386

Comparison is toxic to the creative process.
Stop yourself from doing this. Appreciate
your unique approach.

387

Close your eyes. Then open them and use the first thing you see to spur a creative project.

388

If you could be any person, who would it be and why?

389

Get to know every painting in your favorite museum, even if it takes a lifetime of visits.

390

Describe your creative project to someone who knows nothing about it.

391

There is wisdom in the old proverb
"Nothing ventured, nothing gained."

392

Set up a time each morning when you do
creative work before you get started
on "regular" work.

393

Sharing your creative work, your process,
your passions, your wonder can help
ideas develop.

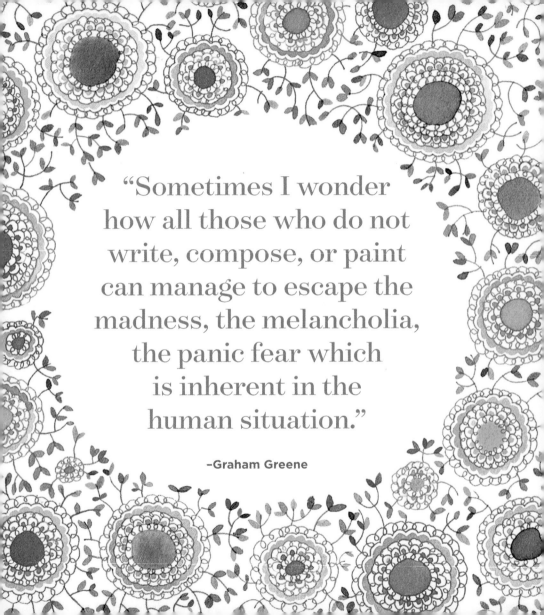

"Sometimes I wonder how all those who do not write, compose, or paint can manage to escape the madness, the melancholia, the panic fear which is inherent in the human situation."

–Graham Greene

394

Imagining how the elements of a creative work
can be rearranged sharpens your creative thinking.

395

Send yourself an entire floral arrangement
to celebrate a creative achievement.

396

Asking questions means you are
always seeking inspiration.

397

Start a reading group.

398

Write about the last kiss of an ended relationship.

399

Compile a book of unique recipes.

400

Record how you spend your time for a week.
Look at how much time was spent in activities
that enriched your life and creativity.

401

Pick a random destination and hop on
the first affordable flight, train, or bus.
Write about the adventure.

402

Every piece of criticism is an opportunity
for advancing new work.

403

Lie on your back and draw what you see.

404

Try alla prima, the act of finishing
a painting in one sitting.

405

If you won a free ticket to anywhere,
where would you go and why?

406

Just as the projects of others inspire you, your projects can inspire others. Put your work out there and see what comes back to you.

407

Take a vacation at a cooking school.

408

What fortune would you like to get in a fortune cookie?

409

Ask for the kind of criticism you want. Or don't ask at all.

410
Design a cross-stitch or embroidery pattern.

411
Work at your own pace. Don't impose
pressure on your creative process.

412
Allow yourself to work on multiple
projects at once.

413
What books would you read to prepare
for writing your own book?

"Speak little.
Do much."

–Benjamin Franklin

414

Paint an outdoor scene on a random piece of junk, like driftwood or an old car door.

415

Be proactive. Generate your own work and opportunities.

416

Create a fragrance from essential oils and give it a sexy name.

417

What are the most creative adventures you have experienced?

418

Upgrade your computer software if it will
make your creative work easier.

419

Give someone a drawing of your own creation.

420

Write down 10 practical and 10 impractical things
to do right now that would give you pleasure.

421

Love the strange feeling you get
when a work of art speaks to you.

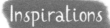

Create Things That Make You Happy

A bonsai forest

Christmas cards

Comic strips starring your family and friends

A compost area in your yard

A coupon booklet of favors as a gift for someone

Dot art

An Etch A Sketch masterpiece

A family scrapbook

A fictional character with an intriguing name

A finger paint masterpiece

Fractal art

A fun hairdo

A gourmet meal

A hand-drawn typeface

A homemade cake or pie

An item of clothing made from newspaper

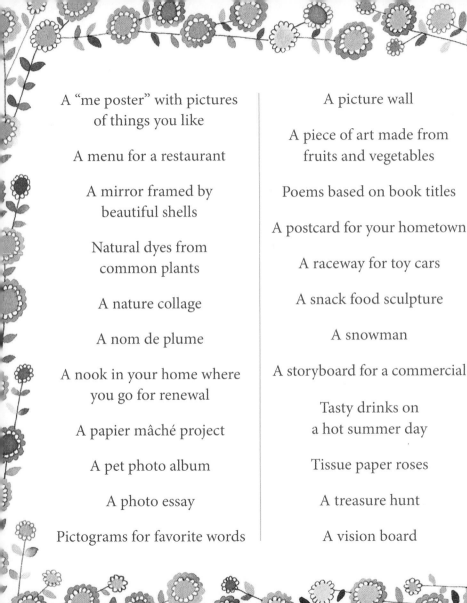

A "me poster" with pictures
of things you like

A menu for a restaurant

A mirror framed by
beautiful shells

Natural dyes from
common plants

A nature collage

A nom de plume

A nook in your home where
you go for renewal

A papier mâché project

A pet photo album

A photo essay

Pictograms for favorite words

A picture wall

A piece of art made from
fruits and vegetables

Poems based on book titles

A postcard for your hometown

A raceway for toy cars

A snack food sculpture

A snowman

A storyboard for a commercial

Tasty drinks on
a hot summer day

Tissue paper roses

A treasure hunt

A vision board

422

Follow any new passion that beckons to you.

423

Think about 10 boring chores you could be doing instead of creating. That should keep you focused on your project!

424

Create a themed room in your house.

425

Throw caution to the wind when you experiment with a new recipe.

426

Transform your garage into a workshop
or a practice space for your band.

427

Do string painting.

428

Write about something you believed for
a long time that you no longer believe.

429

Look for the unusual in everything you do.

430

Check out sections of a bookstore
that you have never visited before.

431

Head toward a new frontier without a map.

432

The next time you get the urge
to do something outrageous
(and unharmful), give in and do it.

433

Be curious.

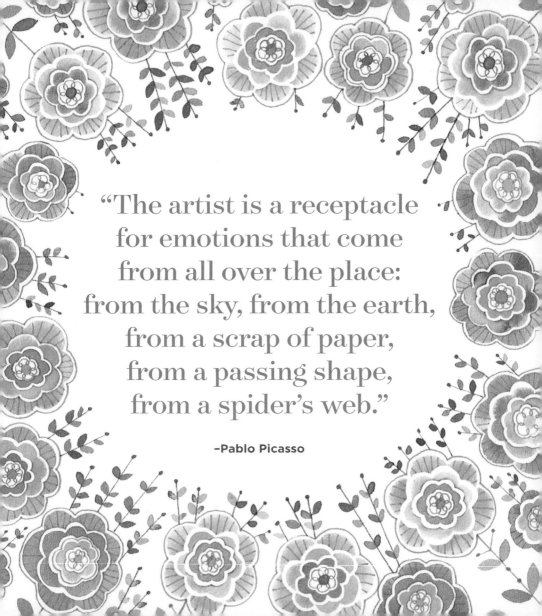

"The artist is a receptacle for emotions that come from all over the place: from the sky, from the earth, from a scrap of paper, from a passing shape, from a spider's web."

–Pablo Picasso

434
Take a pottery class.

435
Cultivate your side projects.

436
Draw an entire building without lifting
your pencil until it's done.

437
Eliminate from your life that which does not
fulfill you spiritually, emotionally, or creatively.

438

Run around your neighborhood to clear
your mind and jump-start your energy.

439

Draw a still life of objects in your house,
such as a wine bottle and pieces of fruit.

440

Take pictures of all the projects you create.

441

Make a recipe with a spice you have
never used before.

442

Pretend to be a travel writer when you are
on vacation. Take notes on every experience
and then write an article.

443

Tell a visual history of your life through
meaningful objects, pictures, and writings.

444

How could you inexpensively make your
home or office more beautiful?

445

Seek out affordable art at street fairs
or on the Internet.

Get the Creative Juices Flowing

Be an archaeologist of life, studying the history and culture behind everyday happenings.

Stop, look, and really listen.

Close your eyes and grab 10 random Scrabble tiles. Try to make a word out of the tiles and then use that word as an idea for a project.

Play with Legos, Play-Doh, crayons—anything that helps get your mind into a more creative space.

Alter your daily routines.

Change the time of day that you exercise.

Try something you have always been curious about. Right now.

Observe a day of silence.

Believe in yourself. Your subconscious will let the best ideas float to the surface.

446
Don't do things in the usual way.

447
The best way to get approval is to not need it.

448
Turn off the television. Use that time to create!

449
Learn enough of a foreign language to order a meal.
Try out your skills at a local ethnic restaurant.

450
What are the elements of your perfect creative day?

451
Think of creativity as a religion.
Carry it with you every day and let it
guide all of your actions.

452
Find that extra hour in the day that
belongs to nobody else but you.

453
Doodle.

454

Make a picture of weather happening in an
odd place, like a snowstorm in a barn.

455

Keep a curiosity file. Reexamine this once a month.

456

Decorate a wreath with objects that are
meaningful to you.

457

Summarize each day with a poetic sentence.

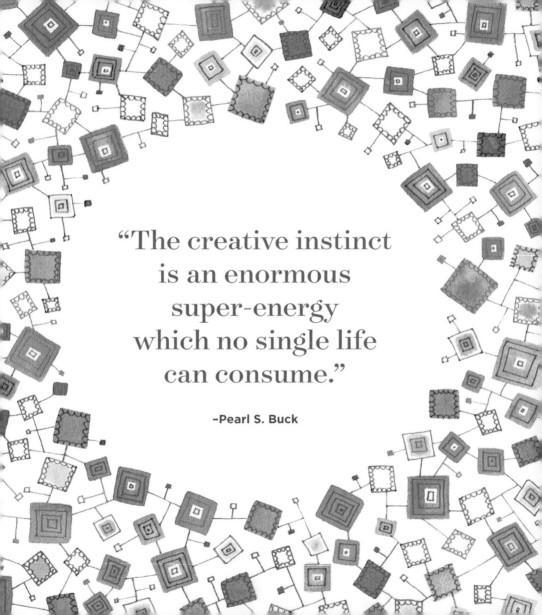

"The creative instinct
is an enormous
super-energy
which no single life
can consume."

–Pearl S. Buck

458
Ride your bike a little farther than normal.
See what you discover.

459
Make original holiday cards.

460
Can you riff off of projects you used to do
and switch creative gears?

461
You will make progress by sticking your
neck out and taking initiative.

462

Reversing your point of view is a good technique for opening up your thinking.

463

See the world differently by walking before dawn or after dark if you feel safe.

464

Use sealing wax as a dramatic way to end a letter.

465

What would you do if you did not have to do it perfectly?

466

Instead of being impatient in a waiting room,
long line, or heavy traffic, take the time to rest
your head and let your mind relax.

467

Produce multimedia shows on your computer.

468

Free your mind to the worlds of fantasy
and imagination.

469

Observe the death of a flower bouquet.
Can you see the beauty in its demise?

470

List 10 to 20 things you enjoy doing.
Schedule one of these activities per week.

471

Dust off an old idea and make it happen.

472

Redesign an everyday object that could
use some improvement.

473

Imagine the world from your pet's point of view.

474

Listen to music you love as you create.

"The creative mind plays with the objects it loves."

–Carl Jung

475

Who is your favorite fictional character?
Why is this your choice?

476

Write an essay about why you moved
to your current hometown.

477

In a word, sentence, or drawing,
re-create a memory from each year
you have been alive, as far back
as you can remember.

478

Identifying an area of focus is a doorway
to a new path. Savor the journey.

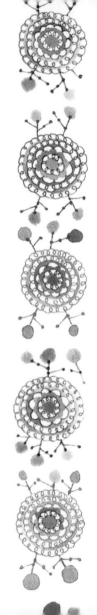

479

Once you get the creativity bug,
it never goes away.

480

Make a flip-book of something you
find enjoyable or humorous.

481

Design a fantasy city.

482

See everything around you as if it is
part of a movie set.

483

Learn to write by writing.

484

Be deeply affected by experience.

485

What do you have to lose by living fully
and well?

486

Use a favorite melody as a starting point
for a creative project.

487

Grasp inspiration from a dream.

Take Time to See the Details of Everyday Life

What is the first thing you think about in the morning?

What details do you notice about your breakfast food?

What sensory experiences stand out during
your morning routine?

Notice the conversations you have in your mind.

At what time do you start thinking about lunch?

During which part of the day are you most energetic?

How do you feel when you think about heading home
for the evening?

What pre-bedtime rituals help you sleep better?

What details can you recall about yesterday?

What were the highlights of today?

488
Revise!

489
Put new photographs in all your picture frames.

490
The shape of your life depends
on what you make time for.

491
How would you like to contribute creatively
to the world during your lifetime?

492
Draw a map of an imaginary place.

493

What do you remember best from your childhood summers? Are the memories tied to new experiences?

494

Change your look for one day.

495

A thesaurus can be a writer's treasure trove.

496

Open a drawer and draw its contents.

497

Sign up for a creative workshop.

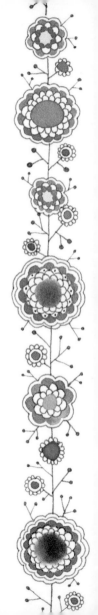

498

Invent new holidays for your family.

499

Write about being in a place that
no one has seen before.

500

Stop to meditate and breathe for
three seconds rather than rushing on.
What can you find in a pause?

501

Refuse to compromise your ideals and
values while pursuing the life you want.

"This world is
but canvas to our
imaginations."

–Henry David Thoreau

502

Borrow from old-fashioned styles,
architecture, industries, and eras.

503

Instead of talking and talking and talking
about your project idea, just get started.

504

Study the meanings and histories of colors.

505

Recognize when you are burning out.
Take a break to recharge and become
inspired again.

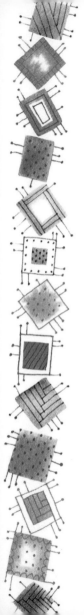

506
Determine your own standards
for creativity.

507
Make colorful ice pops.

508
Watch an improvisation group.

509
Design an amazing postage stamp.

510
Be constantly, quietly aware.

511

Can you turn a current event into
a creative project?

512

Check the back of your mind—your back
burner—for any ideas lurking.

513

Introduce yourself to new concepts by
auditing a class at a local college.

514

Creative people believe they are creative,
so they create.

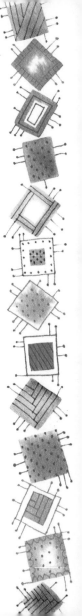

Inspirations

Design Anything in Your World

An advertising campaign for a cause you believe in

The boat you wish you could own

A briefcase

A chair

Doghouses and cat perches

A family flag

Jewelry

A lamp

A museum exhibit

A music album cover

A new household appliance

A patio

A peaceful bedroom

The perfect bed

A purse or wallet

Stationery

A themed calendar

A unique house

A website

A wedding gown

Your dream house

Your ideal kitchen

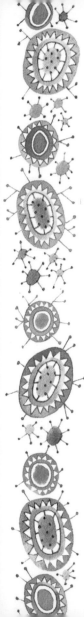

515
Write a few personal thoughts in a notebook
before starting your day.

516
Read books about innovative problem-solving.

517
Design your own purse or wallet.

518
Watch a cat as it watches things outdoors.
Narrate what the cat is thinking.

519

Make a list of things you will never do
before you die.

520

Draw ideas or feelings that are too imprecise
to fit into the "reducing lens" of words.

521

Be resilient. See failure as an opportunity to learn.

522

Often you have to break out of one pattern
to discover another one.

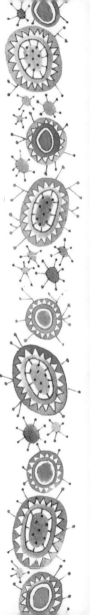

523
The first step to controlling your destiny
is to imagine it.

524
Put on a puppet show. Create the puppets
and characters, and design the set.

525
Make a list as long as your arm.

526
Draw your pet while it is sleeping.

"They're only crayons.
You didn't fear them
in kindergarten,
why fear them now?"

–Hugh MacLeod

527
Choose companions who encourage
your creativity.

528
Write a science fiction story.

529
Record a book on tape for a blind person.

530
Build a winterized hideaway above the garage.

531
Feel the need to scream? Channel the artist
Edvard Munch and draw your rage.

532

Pretend you are floating down the Amazon River.

533

Do karaoke.

534

Create a new Pinterest board.

535

Draw a picture of the night sky,
mapping the stars you see.

536

Draw the moon as if you were on it.

537
Name your house.

538
Create and stock your own backyard pond.

539
Are you afraid to call yourself creative?
What part of the word's definition do you
believe you don't fulfill?

540
Create a landscape painting of your
favorite scene in town.

541

Incubation of ideas often happens when you
are not trying. So allow your brain to rest.

542

If you have a smartphone, you have
a full multimedia studio at your disposal.

543

Do a tin-can craft.

544

Try taking photographs from unusual angles.

545

Treasure and nurture the abilities
that come naturally to you.

546

Figure out what creativity means to you.

547

Design your own logo. Get it printed
on business cards and stationery.

548

You can never be sure about any step you take.
But if you do nothing, nothing will happen.

549

Creatively lace your shoes.

550

Play Simon Says.

551

Draw what different scenes would look like
if viewed from the top of a tree, from the level
of a blade of grass, or from a hole in the ground.

552

Try to get through a whole day
without saying yes or no.

553

Design your dream boat.

554

Clear out your physical spaces and
mental clarity comes along.

"We travel because we need to, because distance and difference are the secret tonic of creativity. When we get home, home is still the same. But something in our mind has been changed, and that changes everything."

–Jonah Lehrer

555

Read collections of letters to spur new ideas.

556

Sketch places you have lived, visited, studied, and worked to help retrieve forgotten ideas.

557

Choose a creative project with the express purpose of learning something about yourself.

558

Make dates with yourself to read, dream, and be alone.

559
Make a coin-rubbing picture.

560
Fill a page with pencil graphite. Then use an eraser to "draw" on the page.

561
Use your favorite word in all of your conversations today.

562
Keep an inspiration box of articles, ads, artwork, photos, and anything else that sparks your creativity.

563
Make a comic strip of your life.

564
To grow, you have to take risks.

565
Draw something that is messy or disorganized.
Try to capture its chaotic energy.

566
Figure out where you most often get your ideas.
Return to this well frequently.

567

Let go of the fantasy of perfection.

568

Set aside a half hour to do nothing.

569

Arrange to have dinner with the most
interesting person you know.

570

Write to have a little control over your world,
re-creating it more to your liking.

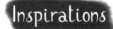

Build In a Transition Between Work and Creative Time

Work out.

Walk around the block.

Take a nap.

Play with the kids.

Hang out with your partner.

Meditate.

Listen to music.

Shower and change into comfortable clothes.

Cook dinner.

Read a book.

Take a bike ride.

Water your garden.

571

Draw a person sitting in a café or library.
Do 10 of these life drawings over several weeks.

572

Change your routine and your surroundings
to help unblock your mind.

573

Decoupage a planter.

574

Rename the planets.

575
Experiment with new outfits.

576
Notice things that are easy to overlook.

577
Although it may be offbeat or unusual,
often the second "right" answer is
a great way to solve a problem.

578
Resist the obvious.

579

Become absorbed in a Japanese landscape
painting. See how the open spaces
invite the viewer into the scene.

580

Imitate a voice from a cartoon.

581

Come up with a family motto.

582

Invent an activity that would inspire
creativity in others.

583

Make up some knock-knock jokes with a kid.

584

Create an incentive for finishing a project.
Maybe you can eat at your favorite restaurant
when you complete your first chapter.

585

Try your hand at fashion design.

586

Return to a creative outlet you had earlier
in your life. See what happens now.

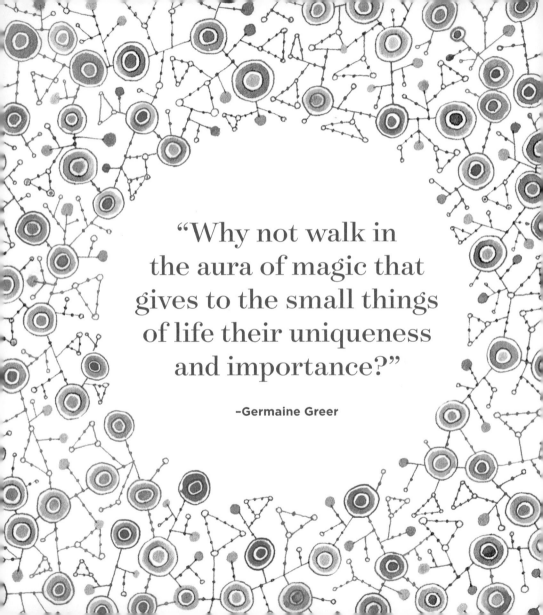

"Why not walk in
the aura of magic that
gives to the small things
of life their uniqueness
and importance?"

–Germaine Greer

587
Sometimes a creative block has nothing to do
with the project. Maybe you have an
unresolved problem or an apology
to deliver. Look for a solution.

588
How much time can you give to creative pursuits
each week? This is a goal to work toward,
but always be prepared to deal with changes.

589
Craft new poems based on the titles
of existing poems.

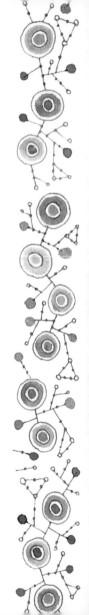

590
Invent a new dance move.

591
Be the mysterious writer in a fancy café.

592
Help a group of students write
and produce an original play.

593
Invent new ways to love.

594
Dress in colorful clothes.

595

Make a home for yourself inside your own head.

596

Use popular culture to inspire your work.

597

Do not filter your brainstorms.

598

Make a list of all the major world events
that you can recall. Does this provide
fodder for a creative project?

599

Create a color-coordinated dinner, such as red, white, and blue food for the Fourth of July.

600

Can you play any songs on an instrument? Try to expand your repertoire.

601

Serenade someone you love, knowing it is the thought that counts.

602

The creative person usually has two kinds of jobs: one that pays the bills and the other that is creative.

603
Participate in a group art project.

604
Put aside judgment, preconceived notions, and fears. These stand between you and creative fulfillment.

605
Sit on the living room floor, crank up the music, and draw cool things you have seen in magazines and books.

606
Challenge any "boundaries" you have been abiding by, consciously or unconsciously.

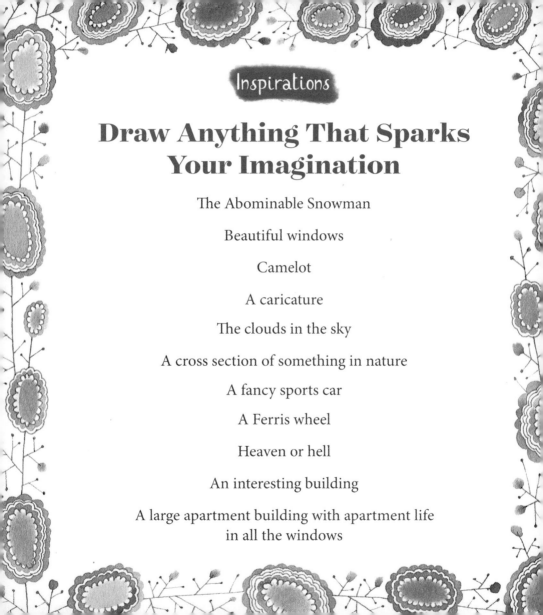

Draw Anything That Sparks Your Imagination

The Abominable Snowman

Beautiful windows

Camelot

A caricature

The clouds in the sky

A cross section of something in nature

A fancy sports car

A Ferris wheel

Heaven or hell

An interesting building

A large apartment building with apartment life
in all the windows

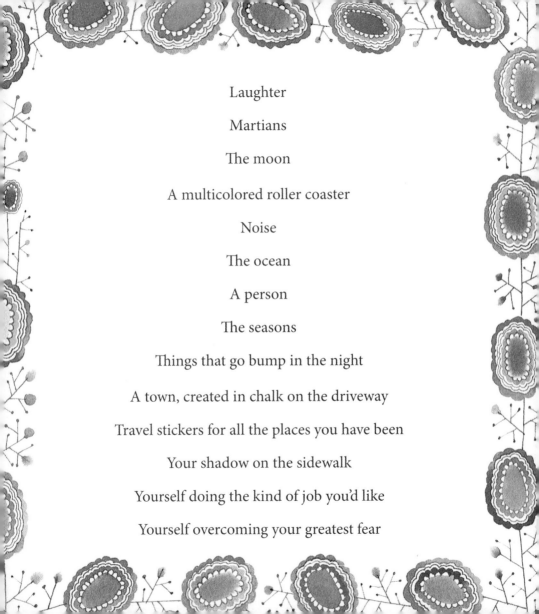

Laughter

Martians

The moon

A multicolored roller coaster

Noise

The ocean

A person

The seasons

Things that go bump in the night

A town, created in chalk on the driveway

Travel stickers for all the places you have been

Your shadow on the sidewalk

Yourself doing the kind of job you'd like

Yourself overcoming your greatest fear

607

What was your best idea ever? How did you get that idea and what happened just before it?

608

Explore a hidden world under a log.

609

Make a pinhole camera.

610

Take up oil painting.

611

Dance to zydeco.

612

Make dog biscuits from scratch.

613

Imagine yourself doing the kind of job
you'd like "when you grow up."

614

Do a trip journal.

615

Create an artistic map of your favorite street.

616

Collect a few simple objects from the outdoors.
Play with combining them or taking them apart.
Does this give you ideas to build on?

617

Explore quiet back roads without a plan.
Breathe deeply and let inspiration come to you.

618

Make art with another person.

619

Design a silly hat.

620

Stand at one unique spot in the universe,
at one moment in the expanse of time,
holding a blank sheet of paper.
What will you write?

621

Create something while you're doing laundry.

622

Describe your favorite teacher. Chances are he or she inspired you in some unforgettable way.

623

Sing Christmas carols.

624

Sew a pillowcase from old shirts.

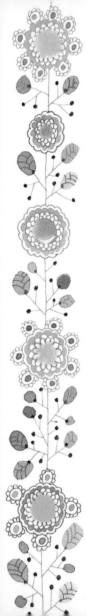

625
Build an elaborate sandcastle.

626
Write a screenplay.

627
Learn to play in the pauses of life.

628
Make a sandwich that is a layered piece of art.
Remember to take a picture of it.

629
What activity makes you feel alive?

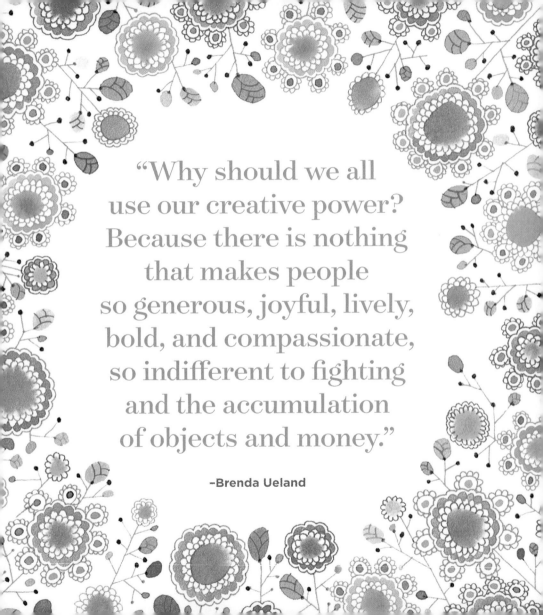

"Why should we all
use our creative power?
Because there is nothing
that makes people
so generous, joyful, lively,
bold, and compassionate,
so indifferent to fighting
and the accumulation
of objects and money."

–Brenda Ueland

630

Keep personal details to yourself.
Instead cultivate a mysterious personality,
leaving much to the imagination.

631

What can you do with a roll of white paper,
crayons, and imagination?

632

Titles that people have chosen for songs,
paintings, and books are rich
in poetic possibility.

633

Draw the country house you hope
you will live in one day.

634
Design jewelry.

635
Paint a room in your favorite color.

636
What tools would you like to have for your creative work? Save up for something you can really use.

637
Apprentice with somebody.

638
Write a letter to your descendants.

639

Creating art it is a form of being
totally present in the moment.

640

If someone else can do it, so can you.

641

Ask how you can make a better world.

642

Rearrange the furniture.

643

Watch a children's cartoon.

644

Build a nest and see if a bird comes to claim it.

645

Just pick up a pencil and begin.

646

Use acrylic paint or permanent markers
to decorate a pair of canvas shoes.

647

Write a haiku that celebrates life.

648

Learn how to build a canoe.

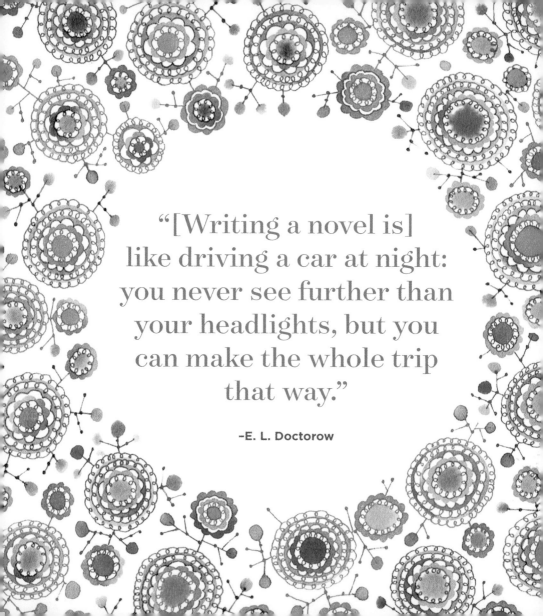

"[Writing a novel is]
like driving a car at night:
you never see further than
your headlights, but you
can make the whole trip
that way."

—E. L. Doctorow

649

Decorate a box to keep your treasures in.

650

Stage an action figure battle with
your favorite child.

651

Think of the possibilities if you mix
analog and digital work.

652

Cross over to another medium. If you
usually write, try painting. If you paint,
try working with clay or playing
a musical instrument.

653
Write a letter to the most important person
in your life to be delivered in the
event of your death.

654
Compose a school song.

655
Make smiley face pancakes.

656
Invent a new buzzword.

657
Expose yourself to great works of music.

658

Paint diagrams of the heavens on dark paper
with luminous paint.

659

To create freely, judgment must be set aside.

660

Write quiz questions about a subject
you are wrestling with.

661

Do something frivolous.

662

Knit a sweater.

663
Be like George Costanza from *Seinfeld*
and do everything opposite for a day.

664
Stage a trivia night with your friends.

665
Make up a new jelly bean flavor.

666
Build your own skylit studio in the woods.

667
Write a play.

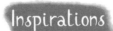

Take Cues From Nature

Look for five beautiful natural objects outside your home.

Take a walk in the woods. Create a color scheme
from the natural items you see along the way.

At the beach, make a palette from the colors in plants,
driftwood, shells, and the sand.

Study the shapes and textures in rocks, minerals,
the peaks of mountains, or the curve of a hill.

Appreciate the meteorological forces at work every day.

Study the way the moon casts shadows and the
stars glint in the night sky.

Look at the shape, colors, and textures of flowers.

Listen to the musical sounds of nature—driving rain,
wind in a primeval forest, waves striking a beach.

668

Remember that there is no "right" starting place.

669

Leave a little bit unfinished for the next day.
It is easier to get started after letting
a project marinate.

670

Carry a notebook or sketchbook to museums
and galleries.

671

Write a story about the best night of your life.

672

Design a roller coaster.

673

The point of learning is growth.

674

Spend a day off the grid.

675

Open an encyclopedia to a random page and read
an entry. What can you do with this new knowledge?

676

Paint a glass plate as an art project.

677
Build a telescope.

678
For a half hour, use no words, only signs and gestures. Think about how you can employ visuals to communicate.

679
Watch a caterpillar transform into a butterfly.

680
Invent a new flavor of lollipop.

681
Jazz up some sneakers with wacky shoelaces, glitter, buttons, or markers.

682
Imitate everyday sounds.

683
Organize a skit night.

684
Dabble in something you know
nothing about.

685
To jump-start your writing,
draft the part that is bursting
to get out of you.
Then go back and add the rest.

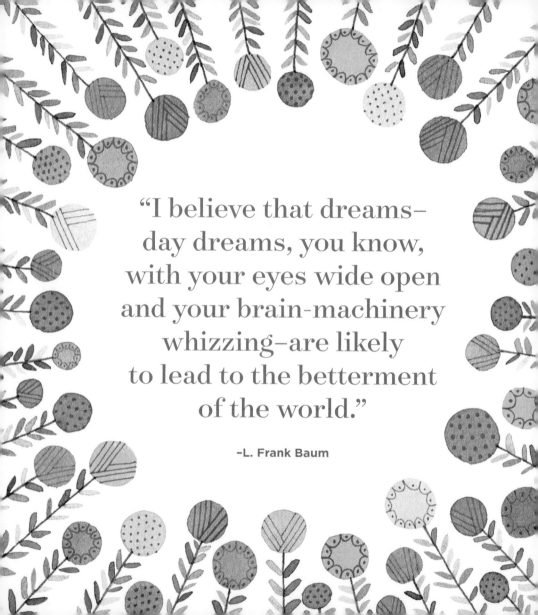

"I believe that dreams–
day dreams, you know,
with your eyes wide open
and your brain-machinery
whizzing–are likely
to lead to the betterment
of the world."

–L. Frank Baum

686

Read a how-to book about a hobby
you would like to pursue.

687

Cleaning up your workspace helps
unclutter your mind.

688

Set up a family art show or performance
in your driveway.

689

Every creative person starts with an empty page,
blank canvas, or lump of clay.

690
Use your heart, your billions of neurons,
your own two hands.

691
Attend bizarre lectures.

692
Sign up for whimsical classes.

693
Become a scrapbooker.

694
Ask an artistic friend to take you to his
or her favorite gallery.

695
Aim high and take chances.

696
Pause. Let your mind go where it wants.
Then take a deep breath and come back
to your project.

697
Make a list of things you would like
to create in your lifetime.

698
Look at grooming as the art of practicing
creativity on your own body.

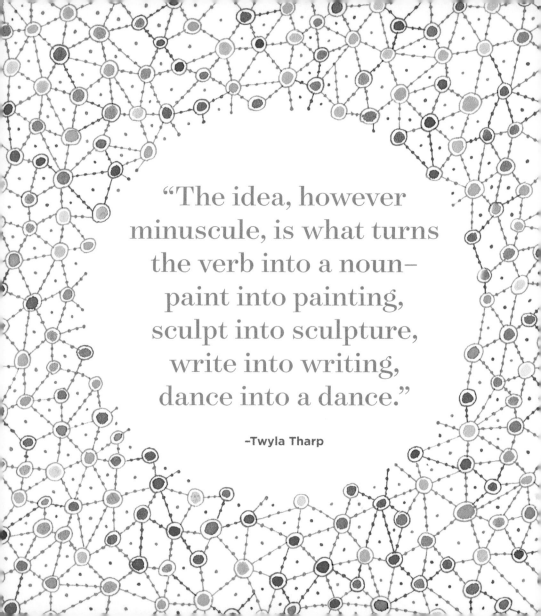

"The idea, however minuscule, is what turns the verb into a noun– paint into painting, sculpt into sculpture, write into writing, dance into a dance."

–Twyla Tharp

699

Take notes for your autobiography.

700

Imitate an improvisational jazz musician.

701

Go on a drawing retreat.

702

Send a small, whimsical gift to brighten someone's long day.

703

Stage a pet parade.

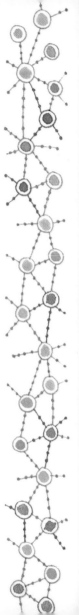

704
Pretend to be a secret agent for a day.

705
Sign up for a watercolor workshop.

706
Remember that whenever your mind expands,
it never shrinks back to its original dimensions.

707
Dive in and dig deep.

708
Draw an item from the inside out.

709
Walk in one direction for as long as you can,
until a brilliant idea comes to you.

710
Experiment with life as you do with art—
mix different ingredients and
try new formulas.

711
Decorate a juice can and use it to plant seeds.

712
Create a homemade musical instrument.

Inspirations

Make Things With Your Hands

An Advent calendar

A bark rubbing with paper and crayons

A bird feeder

A box for viewing an eclipse

A catnip toy

A centerpiece for dinner

A ceramic cup or bowl

Clever luggage tags

Coasters

A collage from leftover grocery products

A cootie-catcher

A crown of flowers

A day-in-the-life video of your family

A "Do Not Disturb" door hanger or a doorstop

A leaf stencil

A life-size replica of yourself

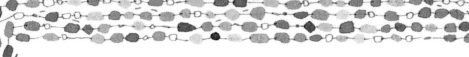

A list as long as
your arm

A loaf of bread

A marionette

A maypole

A Möbius strip

Paper flowers

Party favors and
place cards

A piñata

A pinwheel

A pot holder or hot-plate pad

A rain gauge

A recipe with only
four ingredients

Relief maps

A scrapbook with
words and images

Sponge paintings

A sundial

A stained-glass window
made with tissue paper

A tire swing

Unique folders or
folder tabs
with pictures

Wax pressings of leaves
and flowers

713
Pretend you have the starring role
in a soap opera.

714
Stage an in-home concert.

715
Start an annual writers' retreat, even if
it's just a few creative friends spending
a weekend honing their craft.

716
Play with the art of limerick, a humorous,
frequently bawdy verse of three long
and two short rhyming lines.

717

Write about an artwork by your favorite master artist.

718

Create your own website or blog.

719

Commit yourself to a certain amount of time invested solely in furthering your artistic growth.

720

Live each weekend by whim.

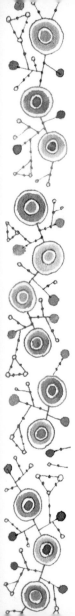

721

Notice that writers often invite readers
to generate their own sense of meaning.

722

Today do something different, enlightened,
creative, imaginative, compassionate,
wise, or fresh. You will become
addicted to this feeling.

723

Start a dream diary.

724

Sketch a scene at 8 a.m. Return 12 hours later
and sketch it again.

"Don't loaf and invite inspiration; light out after it with a club."

–Jack London

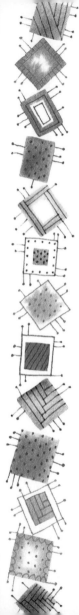

725

Use seven words to say something
beautiful or profound.

726

Control and predictability squash creativity.

727

The first step is always the hardest.

728

Make a list of everything that supports
and nurtures your creative life. Reach for one
of these when inspiration is needed.

729

Pick up a harmonica and breathe into it.
Just play.

730

Write in the margins of your books.

731

Creativity is not nonstop. Be sure to take breaks.

732

Practice perspective drawing: represent the way
objects appear to get smaller and closer
together the farther away they are.

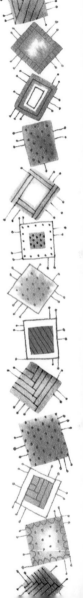

733
Ask a writer friend to take you to one
of their favorite bookstores.

734
Perceive the edges, negative spaces,
relationships and proportions, and lights
and shadows of an object.

735
Creative people find a way to create
wherever they are and no matter
how they are feeling.

736
Engage fear and turn it into energy.

737

Make a table decoration.

738

Decorate a brick for a doorstop.

739

Ask: Why not? What rules can I break?
What assumptions can I drop?

740

Create a new breakfast cereal.

741

Sip piña coladas outside on a beautiful day.
Imagine that you are on a tropical vacation.

Make a Date With Your Inner Artist

Attend a street festival.

See a play.

Drive to a town that you have never explored.

Try a new cuisine.

Go to a concert.

See an art house movie.

Visit a sculpture garden.

Actually use those scrapbooking materials
that are gathering dust in a closet.

Check out old vinyl records at a flea market.

Visit an art gallery.

Pick wildflowers to make a beautiful bouquet.

742

Get lost in music.

743

Wrapping a gift can be an art project.
Go wild and make it beautiful!

744

Build a kite.

745

Construct a pergola in your backyard.

746

Plant tulips in a dazzling array of colors.

747

Paint a T-shirt.

748

Learn how to cultivate a bonsai tree.

749

Learn to identify rocks and minerals
in your environment.

750

Create a build-your-own-sundae bar.

751

How does it feel to let yourself do
something unconventional?

752
Pay attention to changes in your environment.

753
Break the habit of procrastination.
Start now.

754
Spend 10 minutes paying attention
to an object that you think is boring.
Does your thinking change?

755
Invent or reinvent yourself.

756

Trust yourself and your ability to grow
your brainpower.

757

Never leave home without a pen and notebook.

758

Have the courage to follow your talent.

759

Living a balanced life is about learning,
thinking, dancing, playing, creating,
and working some every day.

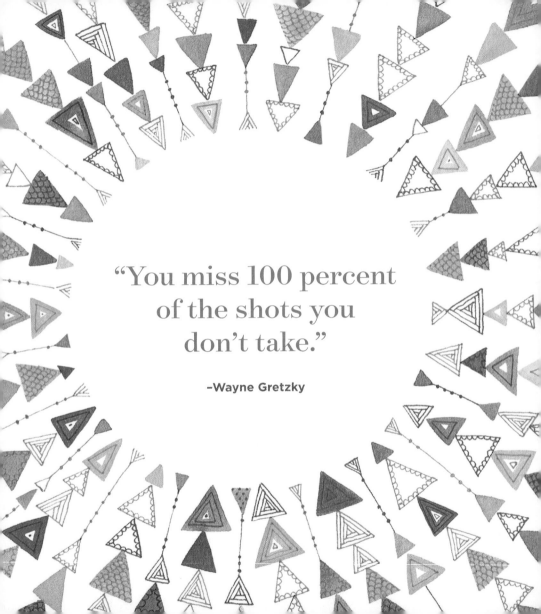

"You miss 100 percent
of the shots you
don't take."

–Wayne Gretzky

760

Explore a culture or foreign cuisine
that calls to you.

761

Draw a favorite room in your childhood home,
including every detail you can remember.

762

At the library, find your favorite fiction
writer's books. Check out a book by an
unfamiliar writer on the same shelf.

763

Design your ultimate desk.

764

Observe, collect, analyze, and compare patterns.

765

Plant yourself somewhere for a half hour.
Observe everything but do not focus on any
single object for more than five minutes.
Write about this experience.

766

Arrange twigs, stack pebbles, and twist
leaves into earth art.

767

Pick a random word out of a thesaurus.
Use it to start a poem.

Ways to Live More Creatively

Cook a meal using leftovers.

Go out for Spanish tapas and taste everything!

Show compassion for coworkers and bosses.

Take a step back when handling a difficult situation or person. Respond instead of reacting.

Learn how to manage pain through meditation.

Use an obscure word you found in a dictionary.

Nickname someone.

Answer emails promptly to minimize their invasion of your time.

Do a little housework each day so you don't spend your entire weekend cleaning.

Take hints for gift-giving.

Fill party-favor bags with dollar-store items.

Create a happy life in your head.

Chuck your to-do list and follow your whims
for a weekend.

Plant an unruly wildflower garden.

Listen, do not speak, when someone tells
you their troubles.

Host a celebration in the most casual way possible.

Use a dinner party as an excuse to try out new recipes.

Travel to a foreign city and attempt to dress
like the locals.

Be happy. Your mood will spread to the rest
of your family.

When one job ends, follow your passions
to the next one.

768
Take things lightly.

769
Rest when you need to.

770
Listen to music that you haven't heard before.

771
Fantasize about your partner.

772
Select a world record that you would like
to break. Make a plan to actually do it!

773

Your favorite play activities tell you
about your authentic self.

774

Make a slide show of family photos
for a special occasion.

775

Learn to play piano.

776

When you are feeling creative, it is easy
to get wound up and overwhelmed with feelings.
Slow down and enjoy the process.

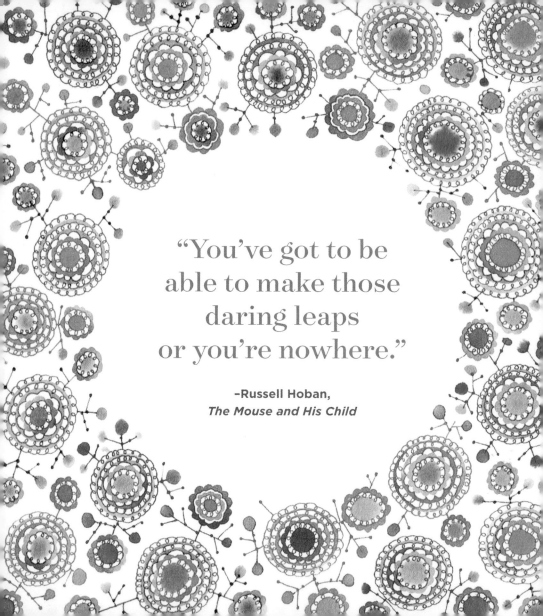

"You've got to be able to make those daring leaps or you're nowhere."

–Russell Hoban,
The Mouse and His Child

777
Take a nature-writing course.

778
Design bridal bouquets.

779
Fill out a time line with your major life events.

780
Seek out opportunities to share ideas:
afternoon coffee klatches, café meetups,
classrooms, creative gatherings,
dinner parties, letters, support
or interest groups, volunteer work, etc.

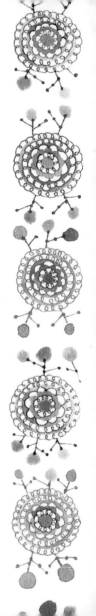

781
Start reading every book you own.

782
Learn about a spiritual tradition that fascinates.

783
Grow a prize-winning vegetable.

784
Draw an original cartoon character.

785
Write a story about stowing away
on a trip to an imaginary place.

786

Build a smartphone app.

787

Figure out what excited you about
a favorite childhood activity.

788

Reread your favorite children's books.

789

Expand your compassion and gratitude
for all people and things in your life.

790
Throw a movie theme party where
each guest dresses as a character.

791
Fight the urge to plan everything. Your creativity
does not thrive under pressure of hurrying,
worrying, and thinking about
what else you should be doing.

792
Many people boast of a great work ethic.
You can also develop a resting
or simply being ethic.

793
Leave your holiday lights up all year round.

794
You have to prepare to be creative.
Figure out what works for you
and make it a habit.

795
Take the long way home.

796
Design cool patches for your clothing.

797
Make a list of the biggest distractions in your life
and do without them for a week.

798
Invent new endings to familiar stories.

799
Tie-dye anything.

800
Build a beautiful dollhouse.

801
Everything is raw material and is
usable and relevant.

"The universe
buries strange jewels
deep within us all,
and then stands back
to see if we can
find them."

–Elizabeth Gilbert

802

Take breaks from multitasking. Increased focus
and awareness will be your reward.

803

Build up a tolerance for solitude—
tranquility without loneliness.

804

Start a recycling project.

805

Build a snow family.

806

Write a letter to yourself to open in the future.

807

Create new palindromes: words or phrases
that read the same backward and forward.

808

Design a botanical garden.

809

Lay out a pamphlet for an activity
you are involved in.

810

Come up with creative storage solutions
in your house.

811

Pretend you are a professional sports announcer
and call every play in your team's next game
(preferably when you are home alone!).

812

Design a new dollar bill or coin.

813

Bring your childhood sense of play
to your everyday life activities.

814

Create beautiful paper fans for a hot summer day.

815

Appreciate humor.

816

Your idea may be crazy, but ask yourself
if it's crazy enough.

817

Tell the devil's advocate in the room to go
back to where he or she belongs.

818

Build a house of cards.

819

Cultivate a rich inner life.

Fancy Yourself a Poet

To get started, try filling out these lines:

My day was _____.

If there was no tomorrow _____.

Time stood still _____.

_____ is under control.

I'm dreaming of a _____.

Nouvelle cuisine _____.

_____ is of great importance.

Midlife crisis _____.

A wild guess _____.

Failure is _____.

You can trust _____.

_____ should never change.

820
Teach yourself to juggle.

821
Ignore the instructions on a craft or science kit.
Construct something completely different
from your imagination.

822
Creativity is not created. It is there
for us to find.

823
Lay out an orienteering course.

824
Configure elaborate tracks for a model train.

825
Invent a new cocktail.

826
Make your home eco-friendly.

827
Compose a piece of music.

828
Use metaphor to connect your past experiences with what is happening now.

829
Know when to stop tinkering.

830
There is no such thing as a cautious
creative person.

831
Your bliss resides in your soul.

832
Remember that it can take decades
for oak trees to produce acorns. There are
many people who do not blossom
until middle age or later. Keep trying.

833

Write a love letter to each member
of your family.

834

Infuse your work with the sublime joy
of living and creating.

835

Keep a journal about your projects.
Write something daily about what you have done
and how you are feeling creatively.

836

Pick a subject or medium that you would
like to explore for a whole year.

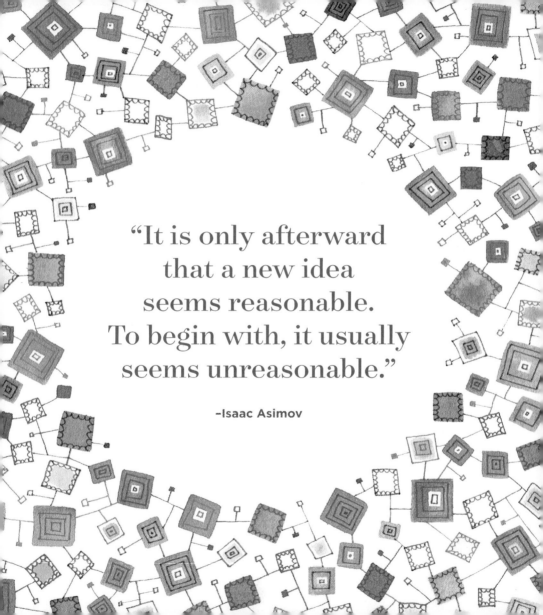

"It is only afterward
that a new idea
seems reasonable.
To begin with, it usually
seems unreasonable."

–Isaac Asimov

837

Make something microscopic that requires
a magnifying glass to see clearly.

838

Carve a bar of soap into an object.

839

Use paint swatches as inspiration.

840

Craft something out of a piece of wood.

841

Do something new every day for a year.
Blog about your 365 new experiences.

842

Don't worry about outcomes.
Enjoy the process.

843

Be selective. What you leave out is as
important as what you keep in.

844

A lively interest in the world around you
is essential for observational drawing
and painting.

845

Take a picture of something that is fleeting—
a bubble, a laser beam, smoke, or sparklers—
then draw or paint what appears in the picture.

846

Along with the learning hand, one must
develop a seeing eye.

847

List things in your house that no one uses.
What else could you do with these items?
Then list things in your house no one
seems to notice. Why is that so?

848
Trace a shadow.

849
Stare at one scene until you get an idea.

850
If money were no object and you could take a few years off, what would you do?

851
Come up with a pseudonym for your mysterious artist self.

Inspirations

Explore New Artistic Media

Acrylic painting

Building design

Ceramic painting

Collage

Colored pencils

Computer animation

Finger painting

Flower arranging

Furniture building

Graphic design software

Knitting or embroidery

Markers

Murals

Musical composition

A musical instrument

Oil painting

Origami

Pastels or charcoal

Poetry

Sculpture

Short stories

Sketchbooking

Tangle or pattern drawing

Videomaking

Watercolor painting

Wood carving

852
Draw in the dark.

853
Write down the best idea you have.
Revisit the idea in 24 hours, in a week,
and in a month. What changes?

854
Experiment with carved book art.

855
Make something out of shredded paper.

856
Write a letter to yourself at another time
in your life.

857

Make a pop-up card.

858

Think up new meanings for
common road signs.

859

Open this book to a random page
and perform one of the entries.

860

Design a flag for a place you love.

861

Be inspired by clouds and trees.

862

Choose six words and create a pictogram
(symbol or simple picture) that describes each.

863

Create a portmanteau: a new word blending two
or more words, like *smoke + fog = smog*.

864

Make a pretty bookmark as a gift.

865

Draw what pleases your eyes.

866
Make a picture frame.

867
Look up words for things you
do not know the names of.

868
Carve a face in a fruit or vegetable.

869
Do something that requires silence.

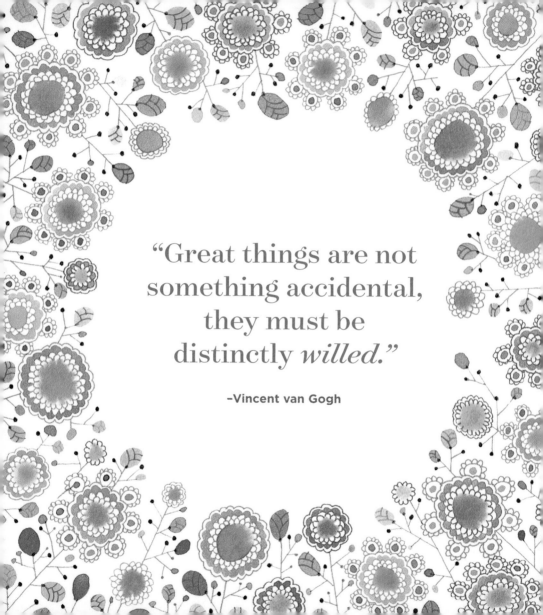

"Great things are not something accidental, they must be distinctly *willed*."

–Vincent van Gogh

870

Paint a holiday scene on a window
(with removable paint).

871

Pick a random event in history
as inspiration for a project.

872

Play with finger paints.

873

Attach a photograph to a larger piece of paper.
Then draw an extension of the photograph
beyond its actual edges.

874

Every time you ask a question that leads
to a creative solution, write it down
so you can use the question again.

875

The real secret to creativity is practice.

876

Learning is a lifelong scavenger hunt.

877

Try listening to a different radio station each day.

878

Give yourself a daily idea quota.

879

Plant a problem in your unconscious.
When you stop trying to solve it,
the answer will come to you.

880

Examine the small universe
of a postage stamp.

881

Trace the lines of cracked pavement.
Use it to make an art piece.

882
Draw butterfly wings.

883
Pay attention to lettering and typefaces on signs, advertisements, menus, and everything else you see. How do the different styles affect the overall feeling of the work?

884
Put on your favorite music and dance!

885
Knowledge is never wasted.

Recognize When You Are in a State of Creative Flow

Your attention is focused and grounded in the present.

What others call loneliness or isolation you call opportunity.

You merge doing with awareness.

Small talk is torture. Disruptors beware!

You become less self-conscious and less self-evaluative.

You see a risk as an exciting invitation.

You sense that you can deal with whatever arises.

You become unaware of time passing.

You experience a creative project as intrinsically rewarding.

When your project is over, you are exhausted in a happy way.

The experience is hard to describe to others.

886
Write your life story in 250 words or less.

887
Grow a fruit tree.

888
Write a plan of action for a business
you want to start.

889
Get a whiteboard and go crazy with graffiti art.

890
Build a radio.

891
Give yourself the space to create,
relax, and think.

892
Create an audacious to-do list, one that
helps you chart your path.

893
Build the ultimate tree house.

894
Write the story of the first time you met
your significant other.

895
Design a computer typeface.

896
Make a sculpture by balancing stones.

897
Mix yellow and blue paint to make bright green.
Then add different amounts of red to see
how many different greens you can create.

898
Make a jigsaw puzzle out of a photograph.

899
Invent a secret code.

900
Design an elaborate hopscotch course
on your driveway.

901
Fold napkins into swans.

902
Create your own silk flower arrangement.

903
Pack a gourmet picnic.

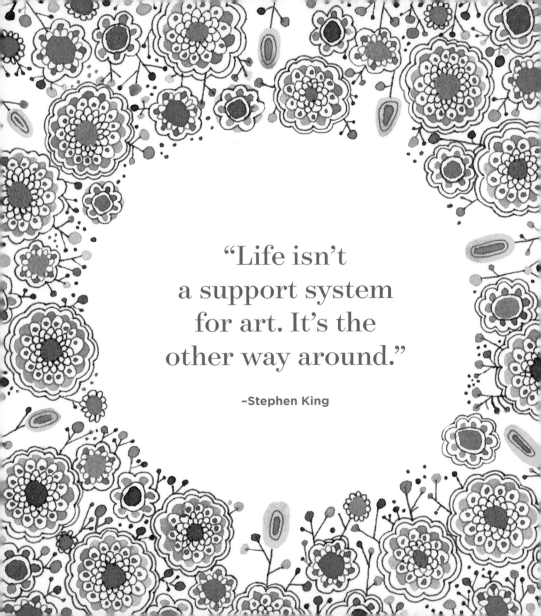

"Life isn't
a support system
for art. It's the
other way around."

–Stephen King

904

Build a miniature village, perhaps
for the holidays.

905

Design a menu for a make-believe restaurant.

906

Teach yourself calligraphy.

907

Try to guess the meaning of an unfamiliar
word from the way it is used.

908
Make a jar terrarium with colored sand,
mini-shells, topsoil, and watercress seeds.

909
Take a defunct object apart to see
what it looks like inside.

910
Weave a friendship bracelet.

911
Make tissue paper roses.

912
Draw what silence looks like.

913
Start a new fad.

914
Make a list of questions you'd like
to know the answers to.

915
Sculpt a block of ice (carefully).

916
Write a sequel to your favorite movie.

917
Create personalized lunch bags.

918
Make a wind chime.

919
Make a guess-the-number-of jar
with seasonal candies.

920
Carry out an art project using
three different media.

921
Make a kaleidoscope.

922
Play a new card game.

923
Write the children's book you
always wanted to read.

924
Create a picnic from a local farmer's market.

925
Customize a crossword puzzle for someone,
providing clues that only you two could know.

926
Design a ring, even your own engagement
or wedding ring.

927
Decorate your mailbox for the holidays.

928
Create a splatter print.

929
Invent the ultimate baked good.

930
Add funny speech bubbles to photos.

931
Design the cover of a book.

932
Design the bathroom of your dreams.

933
Refurbish an old piece of furniture
that has "good bones."

934
Create beauty where you see none.

935
Try everything once.

936
Master a magic trick.

937
Play an observational guessing game,
such as I Spy.

938
Create your own greenhouse.

939
Train a dog to play Frisbee.

940
Make a banner for a celebration.

941
Write a proverb from your own experience.

"Great artists
make the roads;
good teachers and
good companions can
point them out.
But there ain't
no free rides."

–Ursula K. Le Guin

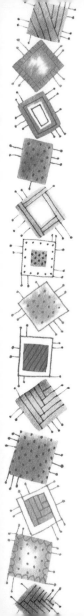

942
Color outside the lines.

943
Create an entire coloring book.

944
Design your own gift baskets.

945
Cut sandwiches into geometric shapes.

946
Make holiday ornaments and decorations.

947

Write a schmaltzy story about
a shipboard romance.

948

Create a family trivia game.

949

Design a calendar as a gift for someone.

950

Fashion a walking stick.

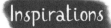
Inspirations

Find Inspiration in the Things You Love

Your family

A favorite piece of jewelry

A stunning art book

The soothing sound of rain

A delicious spice

A fun dance song

The aroma of a homemade meal

Flea markets

Sporting events

The cadence of a foreign language

Your secret hideout

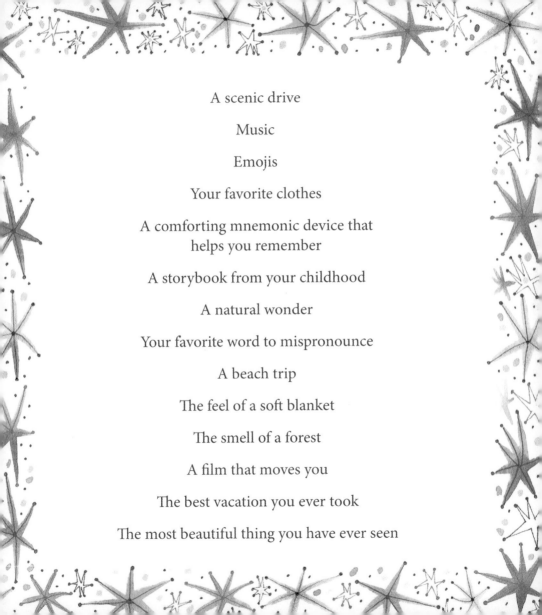

A scenic drive

Music

Emojis

Your favorite clothes

A comforting mnemonic device that
helps you remember

A storybook from your childhood

A natural wonder

Your favorite word to mispronounce

A beach trip

The feel of a soft blanket

The smell of a forest

A film that moves you

The best vacation you ever took

The most beautiful thing you have ever seen

951

Imagine you are the main character
in a book and figure out what
you would have done differently.

952

Discover new trails.

953

Assemble a portable art kit to take with you
on vacation or on days off.

954

Make a list of all the symbols you see in a day.

955

Create "best of" lists at the end of the year.

956

Play Animal, Vegetable, or Mineral.

957

Construct a diorama from leftover
Halloween or Easter candy.

958

Draw an object at an unusual angle
to learn how to capture what you really see,
instead of what your brain expects to see.

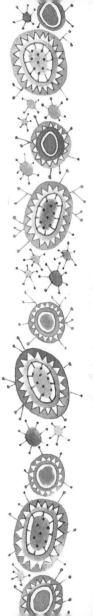

959
Sing a song to the pace of the windshield wipers.

960
For one day, pretend you are living the life
of your favorite TV character.

961
Take 10 pictures of things that have
no pattern or order.

962
Create funny signs for men's and
women's bathrooms.

963
Draw for an hour without stopping.

964
Design one feature you would have
in your home if you had unlimited funds.

965
Make a totem pole.

966
What would be a perfect Happy Meal toy
for grown-ups?

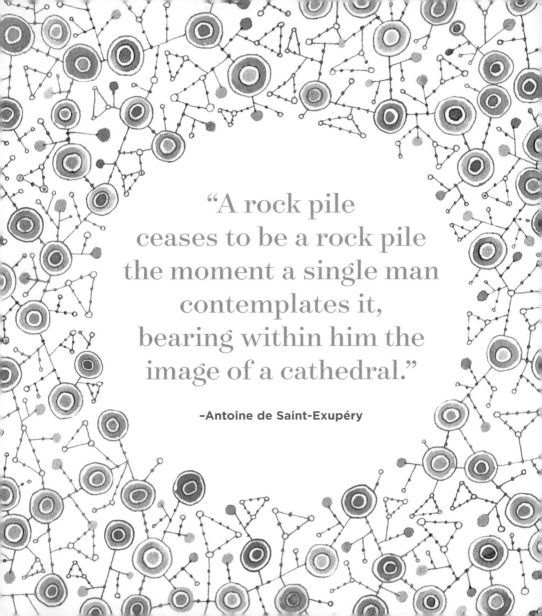

"A rock pile
ceases to be a rock pile
the moment a single man
contemplates it,
bearing within him the
image of a cathedral."

–Antoine de Saint-Exupéry

967

Dream of the places in the world
you want to go.

968

Imagine yourself as an ant pushing
a breadcrumb.

969

Try on crazy clothes at the mall,
just for fun.

970

Draw an interminable staircase.

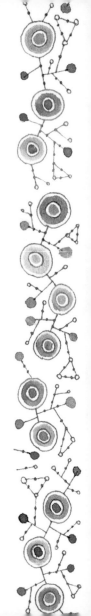

971
Think on your feet. Energy fuels creativity.

972
Walk your dog along a new route.

973
Shop at an ethnic food market.

974
If you were commissioned to build a statue, what would the subject be and where would you erect it?

975
Write about what gives you balance.

976
Compile a list of topics about which you have something to say.

977
Write headlines about yourself.

978
Surround yourself with people, color, sounds, and work that nourish you.

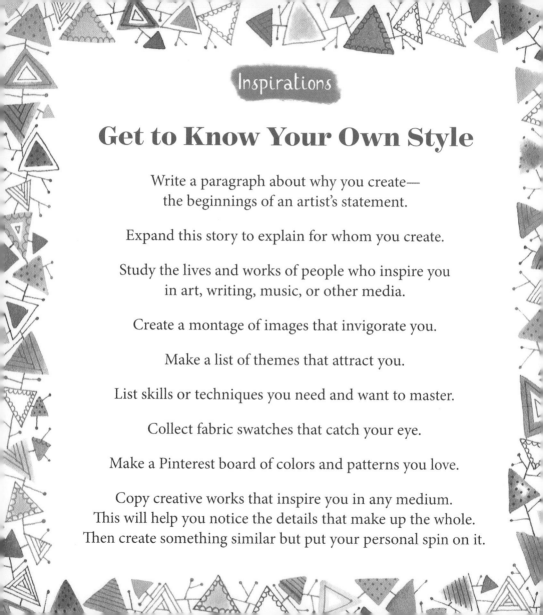

Get to Know Your Own Style

Write a paragraph about why you create—
the beginnings of an artist's statement.

Expand this story to explain for whom you create.

Study the lives and works of people who inspire you
in art, writing, music, or other media.

Create a montage of images that invigorate you.

Make a list of themes that attract you.

List skills or techniques you need and want to master.

Collect fabric swatches that catch your eye.

Make a Pinterest board of colors and patterns you love.

Copy creative works that inspire you in any medium.
This will help you notice the details that make up the whole.
Then create something similar but put your personal spin on it.

979

Treat yourself to a creative bath, with blowing bubbles and special scented soaps.

980

Keep toys on your desk.

981

When you are in the strange, disquieting, chaotic place before you start a creative project, sit with the feeling without judging it or trying to change it. Rest in contemplation. Await the breakthrough to "aha."

982

Write about living in another time period.

983

The most creative ideas will seem
silly at first. Get used to it.

984

Work within limits but do not be
constrained by them. Putting some limits
on a project can help make it doable,
but abandon the ones that get in your way.

985

Write a script for a television show.

986

Create a miniature world with electric trains
and tiny houses, trees, and cars. Make it
the centerpiece of a room.

987

Make up stories about strangers who
walk by on the street.

988

Invent an ice cream with ridiculous ingredients.

989

When playing with a child, let the child
take the creative lead.

990

Channel your hardships and traumas
into your creative work.

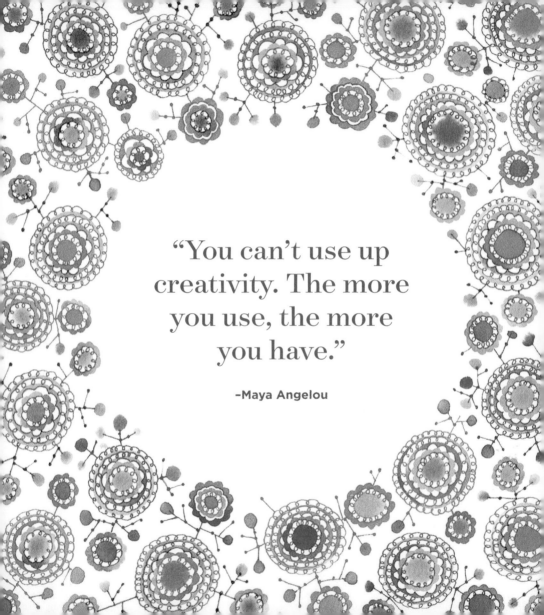

"You can't use up creativity. The more you use, the more you have."

–Maya Angelou

991

Volunteer to build a house for a needy family.

992

It is important to see our choices as
not only one or the other but as a universe
of possibilities and strategies.

993

Don't let fear conquer your creative spirit.

994

Plant a seed. Give it a name and take care
of it every day. Draw how it changes
over time, making one sketch per week.

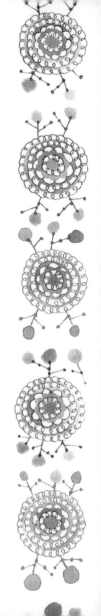

995

Add a calming scent to your favorite notebook:
dab it with a drop of perfume or rub spices
or herbs on the pages.

996

Look through a camera's viewfinder to see how
scenes appear when you focus on a small section.

997

Plant a butterfly garden.

998

Re-create an x-ray in the artistic
medium of your choice.

999

Make a "life pie." Draw a circle and divide it into Adventure, Family, Romance, Friends, Play, Spirituality, and Work. Use this to track how your life is divided among the pieces of the pie. It will tell you a very interesting story.

1,000

Be open to experience. It's the strongest predictor of creative achievement.

1,001

No one is watching. So, go for it!

Acknowledgments

Thank you to Francesca Springolo for her creative illustrations, to Bob Amsler for help checking my manuscript, and to Tom Miller for his agentry. Thank you, also, to Hoops the cat. Hoops has taught me to be very creative in entertaining her while I'm trying to work!

About the Author

Barbara Ann Kipfer is a master listmaker and the author of more than 70 books and calendars, including the bestseller *14,000 Things to Be Happy About* (with more than a million copies in print). This is her third title in the 1,001 Ways series, also including *1,001 Ways to Live Wild* and *1,001 Ways to Slow Down*. She writes thesauri and dictionaries, trivia and question books, archaeology reference, and happiness- and spirituality-themed books. A professional lexicographer, she holds Ph.D.'s in linguistics, archaeology, and Buddhist studies. Find out more about Kipfer at thingstobehappyabout.com.

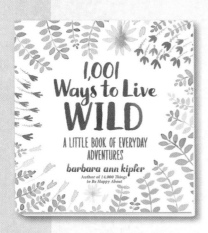

Play in the dirt. Kiss someone in the rain. Plant a garden. Spend an afternoon reading in a hammock. These beautifully illustrated keepsakes give lighthearted words of encouragement and provide practical ideas to help you lead a happy, fulfilled life.